HOW TO RAP 2

ADVANCED FLOW & DELIVERY TECHNIQUES

PAUL EDWARDS

CHICAGO
REVIEW
PRESS

Library of Congress Cataloging-in-Publication Data

Edwards, Paul, 1982–

How to rap 2 : advanced flow and delivery techniques / Paul Edwards ; foreword
by Gift of Gab of Blackalicious.

pages ; cm

Includes index.

ISBN 978-1-61374-401-7

1. Rap (Music)—Instruction and study. 2. Musical meter and rhythm. I. Title.
II. Title: How to rap two.

MT67.E382 2013

782.421649'143—dc23

2013015169

Cover design: Philip Pascuzzo
Cover photographs: iStockphoto
Interior design: Jonathan Hahn

Published by Chicago Review Press, Incorporated
814 North Franklin Street
Chicago, Illinois 60610
ISBN: 978-1-61374-401-7
Printed in the United States of America
5 4 3 2 1

Contents

Foreword

The first experience I had with rhyming was when this one cat would always come down to the building I lived in back in those days—he was older than all of us and he rhymed. He would go off on one person every time he would come through. He would just pick one victim and just start rhyming about them and destroy them, every day. And one day, it was my turn.

He just started coming off the top, talking about my clothes and talking about my hair and all kinds of stuff. After he did that, I went home and wrote a rhyme to battle him. Me and my friend used to ride our bikes to his house every day with papers in our hands, the actual rhymes in our hands, at his front door, and just battle him. So my first rhyme was in self-defense.

He kept killing us, kept killing us, kept killing us—but as I got older and my skill developed, one day I got to a point where I was better than he was. That was really kind of the point where my confidence boosted, like, yeah, you know what, I can do this. That's how I started rhyming.

I think that hip-hop is going in different directions and I think that some younger MCs have different reference points. A lot of the MCs don't know who the Cold Crush Brothers are, don't know who Grandmaster Flash is, some people don't even know who EPMD are, or who Kool G Rap is!

To be a better MC, you need to study people who came before you, and study people that are great, and practice . . . practice. If you're an MC, you gotta write, you gotta create, if you're an artist you have to create. Study people and work hard at it and find your own style, find your own way of how you do it and keep going.

Look to build a body of work, don't look for one hit, look at the bigger picture, look at artists like 2Pac, artists like Miles Davis who just have rows and stacks of records in stores. Look at your career as a body of work, don't look at it as, "I gotta make this hit, if I don't make it, that's it for me, I gotta go do something else."

It's gotta be a lot more than the money—the people who do it long term are the people who love it. If you're looking at it from a long-term perspective, whether you're mainstream or underground, then you have to love it, you have to love what you're doing.

GIFT OF GAB, BLACKALICIOUS

Gift of Gab, of the group Blackalicious, is noted as one of the most dexterous and versatile MCs of all time, using tongue-twisting and varied flows to continually push the boundaries of the art form on each new release, whether on his acclaimed solo records or his classic Blackalicious material. His mastery of flow and delivery put him in an elite category of MCs who can shift effortlessly from one style to another, tirelessly innovating and developing new styles for others to follow.

Introduction

*I like listening to cats that have something to say, but if they're not
saying it in a stylistic or rhythmic way, it's boring and they'll lose
my attention. If we're talking about music, then style outweighs
[content], because music revolves around style and rhythm.*

◄ Myka 9, Freestyle Fellowship ►

Flow and delivery—these are two of the most important elements of MCing, and yet they often remain the least studied and
the least understood. Many people can discuss rap's content and
understand the plot of a story or how clever a metaphor is, but few
people understand things such as triplets, flams, vibrato, staccato
delivery, and other percussive and vocal techniques that are used
in hip-hop music.

Although there is often a focus on content in hip-hop—analyz-
ing it, reviewing it, and criticizing it—for many listeners, fans, and
MCs, content is actually secondary to the flow and delivery, which
give MCing its immediate musical interest. The flow and delivery
are the first aspects of an MC that the listener hears on a song, and
they can make or break an MC.

Brother Ali

I think flow is more important than great lyricism. I think if
you had to have one and not the other, I would always go
with flow over lyricism. There are people whose lyricism
is great, but their flow makes it so I can't listen to them.

Because it's music—at the end of the day, it's music. You're listening to it because of the feeling you get from it and the way that it makes you move and what it does to your soul and your spirit when you hear what's going on. It's music, and [so] before words are even involved in music, it really is about the feel.

Professional MCs have known for a long time how important the flow and delivery are to the actual sound of the music—that's why many of them begin the writing process by coming up with the flow and delivery *first*.

Royce Da 5′9″

I come up with the flow before I write anything down. Once I figure out the flow, then I gotta figure out the words and I just have to figure out how to fit the words into that flow. I usually pick the flow before I even start writing the verse.

Pigeon John

That's definitely the way I do it. A lot of times the melody and rhythm of it comes first, then the [content]. I might hum something, then chop it up in my mind, then fill it in with syllables [later]. So for me, it's more of a musical thing versus a wording thing.

Advanced Techniques

How to Rap 2 provides an in-depth look at flow (rhythm and rhyme) and delivery, giving them the much-needed focus and explanation they deserve, to help MCs take the *sound* of their MCing further and to help hip-hop listeners break down the technical flow and delivery techniques that their favorite MCs use.

This book builds on topics covered in *How to Rap*, greatly expanding and developing them, introducing a huge range of techniques not covered in the first book. *How to Rap 2* is for people who really want to master flow and delivery—MCs who truly want to become another instrument on the track.

Buckshot, Black Moon

Why my flows and my rhythms come out the way they come out is because I become an instrument. If there are five pieces on that beat, I'm gonna be the sixth piece.

This book will give you, the listener, a much more thorough understanding of the level of complexity in MCs' flows, so that you can fully appreciate the level of craft that goes into rhythm, rhyme, and delivery.

This lets you discuss MCing more accurately, so that flow and delivery are looked at as closely as content. Some MCs have a huge level of intricacy in their flow and delivery but have basic content—these MCs should be more fairly judged based on a solid knowledge of flow and delivery techniques.

Aesop Rock

You're always looking for the next pattern or the next rhythm, something that you haven't done—some sort of rhyming stanza that you haven't heard before that you think is very ear catching.

Interviews and Examples

How to Rap 2 uses a combination of exclusive interview quotes and lyric examples to describe the techniques and approaches that the MCs use.

All the quotes in *How to Rap 2* are new, never-before-seen insights from the collection of 104 exclusive interviews conducted with a wide variety of MCs for the first book, as only a fraction of the total material was used in *How to Rap*. A complete list of the MCs quoted in this book begins on p. 223.

Schoolly D

What I do with the artists and the musicians and the poets that I love, I always read their interviews, because that always says something different.

Dray, Das EFX

I learned like everybody else, listening to the ones that came before me. We're students of the game. I'm a big student of the game. Everybody, I think, should always be a student and never be like, "Yo, I got this mastered," because you can always learn some shit. Listen to other MCs out there doing it—you gotta be a student.

In certain cases, it is clearer to use lyric examples to describe the techniques being covered, rather than interview quotes. This is because certain techniques are hard to explain in conversation, especially as many of the terms in this book are either new or are being applied to rapping for the first time. There are lots of rapping techniques that have existed for a number of years but have not been named or focused upon previously.

For example, "flams" (p. 28) occur in percussion but have not been identified in rapping until this book—the technique is used in hip-hop, but no specific terminology has been used to discuss it. As many of these methods have not been put into words before, it's therefore more practical to describe certain things using lyric quotations, often in diagrams that clearly explain the techniques.

Q-Tip, A Tribe Called Quest

Musically you could write it out—you can write out the beats in a bar and pauses and triplets and all of that stuff, show it musically and theoretically, you could apply that to it.

Del the Funky Homosapien

I could write out my flow, for every bar. So then you can visually look at it and see what you're doing.

The Flow Diagram

Lyrics are shown frequently in flow diagrams throughout this book. How flow diagrams work is explained in detail in the first *How to Rap*, pp. 67–79, but here is a brief reminder, as they will be used more extensively in this book.

These are the opening lyrics from the Pharcyde's track "Drop" (00:26), from the album *Labcabincalifornia*, in a flow diagram:

1	2	3	4
Let me freak the	**funk**, obso-	**lete** is the	**punk** that talks
more junk than	**San**ford sells.	I jet pro-	**pel** at a
rate that compli-	**cate** their mental	**state** as I	**in**vade their
masquerade.	They couldn't	**fade** with a	**clip**per . . .

The flow diagram shows us several pieces of information:

- The numbers along the top of the diagram show the 4 beats in a bar of music, so that we can refer to where lyrics fall in relation to the beat (for example "funk" falls on the 2 beat, "-lete" falls on the 3 beat).

- Each new line in the flow diagram represents a new bar of music (the first bar begins "Let me freak the . . ."; the second bar begins "more junk than . . .").

- The syllables that fall directly under the beat numbers are in **bold** type—they are stressed and said in time with the 4 beats in the bar, in order to keep the lyrics in time with the music (such as "Let," "funk," "-lete," and "punk" in the first bar).

- If there is a rest in the flow, then no lyrics fall under that particular beat number (such as the rest on the 3 beat of the second bar just before "I jet pro-" and the rest on the 2 beat of the fourth bar, just before "They couldn't").

As with the first book, the examples are clearer and more easily understood while listening to the song they refer to. For examples in which it will help to hear the track, the time at which the example appears is given after the track name, in this format: (00:00). So an example that occurs one minute and 20 seconds into a song would be shown as (01:20). Timing may vary depending on the version of the track played, so these times are rough guides. Allow for at least several seconds on either side of the time given when listening for the example.

Practice

As with all the elements of being an MC, the key thing with all the techniques in this book is to practice them. Just as no one picks up a guitar for the first time and is able to immediately play all the notes and chords, no one becomes a great MC without practice. This book provides the techniques for you, but you have to practice them.

B-Real, Cypress Hill

Practice as much as you can. It all shows paydirt, man. You'll eventually start hearing how much better you've gotten and people will tell you, "Hey, you sound pretty damn good." All that stuff comes with time and you just have to keep doing it, because progression is everything and the more you do it, the more you progress.

Imani, The Pharcyde

You gotta practice, man. I don't think there's no MC that was dope overnight. Anyone that I can think of as dope, it took time to for it to be fresh, cultivate their sound, cultivate their style, formulate their ideas and shit.

MC Shan

I mean, over time, practice makes perfect, right? And I'm still practicing.

Evidence, Dilated Peoples

Practice—you're not as good as you're going to get, that's the bottom line. That attitude that "I've accomplished it and I've done it" and all that is the worst attitude to have, so don't celebrate too much. Celebrate later.

Even those who believe they have a natural aptitude and talent for rapping have to put in the time and the practice, or they will be overtaken by those who put in more time and effort.

David Banner

Practice. That's the one thing I see with young rappers—they don't practice, they just do it and think that they're good enough. You gotta practice. [For example,] Eminem still writes and writes and writes and writes and writes, that's why he's the Jordan.

R.A. the Rugged Man

It ain't just all natural talent, you really gotta put in the [work] and take that talent and really just fucking keep going and going.

shitty and shallow to say, but I'm going to take a stand and say it. Because I don't care how good [your message is], if I can't feel the way you're saying it, then you should find a different means to translate that message. That's my personal opinion. I mean, think about it—what if a singer had the greatest message but couldn't hit a fucking note? It just doesn't make sense. It's sad to say that "yeah, you have this great message, but no, I don't want to hear you," but it's sad but true.

Omar Cruz

[You] can be saying some phenomenal shit, telling people the secrets to life, but if on the song it's not in the pocket, it's not there, people are gonna be like, "This is wack, this is garbage." I mean, you've heard bad rappers before—you don't care what they'll say, you just go on to the next song, [even though] they can be saying some beautiful shit.

If there is a choice between very clever content on the one hand and staying on time and being properly in the pocket on the other, then staying in the pocket and having great rhythm usually wins out.

Crooked I

I've sacrificed a lot of ingenious metaphors because it wouldn't have fit precisely on the beat how I wanted it to.

Mighty Casey

There's definitely times when I thought of a really clever punch line, but it just didn't work [rhythmically]. So sometimes you have to sacrifice some cleverness on paper for the eventual goal of music and the sound and being pleasing to the ear.

Being on the beat and being able to do interesting things with the rhythm is arguably even more important to sounding good on a track than having a good voice (which is very important in itself, as shown in chapter 2).

Evidence, Dilated Peoples

Would you rather hear someone with a good voice and a bad pocket or someone with a weak voice and good pocket? Rhythm is more important—the pocket.

Vocal Percussion

A lot of the rhythmic techniques in rapping are closer to percussion and drumming than they are to traditional poetic techniques. Although rapping uses a lot of poetic techniques in its content and in some of its rhyme techniques, rhythmically it's very similar to percussion.

Shock G, Digital Underground

I hear and remember the word positions like percussion parts in my head.

Del the Funky Homosapien

I could write out my lyrics like a drum pattern, because I know how to write drum notation, basically. Not gonna say I'm the best, but I could write out a drumbeat if I wanted to, like [the drum break of James Brown's] "Funky Drummer" I could write out on a piece of paper.

This is because rapping almost always has to keep to and maintain a strong beat, unlike poetry, which is often only on the page and can be read in different ways. Therefore, most of the terms in this section come from percussion and drumming rather than poetry analysis. As Mighty Casey says, "Your voice is like a drumbeat on the beat, so every syllable is like a different drum sound."

E-40

I always have been into music. I was in the marching band from the fourth grade all the way to the 12th grade, see, and I played the drums. I was in the percussion, in the drum line, so that's what my thing was, so that's how I did it.

Tech N9ne

Having the rhythm to being able to stay on beat, it made me sort of like a percussionist. I always wanted to play drums, so if you listen to my flow it's like I'm beating on bongos or something.

Thes One, People Under the Stairs

One approach to [coming up with the flow] is to approach it like a producer and hear a rhythm over the beat. Like if we were to add another layer of percussion over this, what would it sound like? And then try to model the rhyme pattern after that.

Writing from the Rhythm

As rhythm is such a key element to making a song sound great, the rhythm is actually where the lyrics begin for many artists—the rhythm is the first thing they come up with, before they even have words for the song. This is touched on in the first *How to Rap* (pp. 113–116), but it bears repeating. Coming up with the rhythm first and making that the initial focus is often the key difference between MCs with advanced flows and those without.

Tech N9ne

I come up with styles first sometimes. I might say I wanna sound like a ping-pong ball on this one, so I'll [come up with the rhythm first and then] put words to it.

Masta Ace

What I do, I'll play the beat and I'll start mumbling words, a flow to that beat. And the words don't make any sense, they just sound like gibberish, but what I'm trying to formulate is how the rhymes that I'm gonna create are gonna flow into that beat. So the beat comes on, and I just start kinda mumbling, and once I get the bounce of how I wanna rhyme, then I start to turn those mumbles into actual words.

Thes One, People Under the Stairs

Now when I sit and hear a beat, I usually flow some nonsense over it until I find some pattern or groove that I really like and then I'll actually put words [to it]. So in a sense I'm getting a syllabic count and I'm getting the pauses and I'm getting that all together in my head and then I actually fit words into it.

Lord Jamar, Brand Nubian

You might just do a flow before you even write the rhyme sometimes, just to test the flow out, and it's meaningless [sounds], you're not even really saying anything.

T3, Slum Village

My method is usually I go into the booth and I come up with a pattern first, or flow. Once I got a flow and I already got the concept, then I match words to the flow.

Focusing on the flow first and coming up with the rhythms before the content means you're putting a lot of thought into and emphasis on how the song will *sound*, rather than what it will mean. This is why a lot of MCs start with the rhythm—they want to get the song to *sound* great before they even begin to come up with a theme or idea for the content.

Stat Quo

You can have great subject matter, but if you don't have a nice flow, people are not gonna want to hear it. Flow is good for the ear—it's something that makes the ear like, "Oh, what is that?" Then when you get the ear, you can put something in there.

K-Os

As a youth, subject matter [was more important to me], but then I'd start doing things like as soon as I got a beat, I'd record, I'd just scat over it. The words wouldn't really mean anything, I'd just get the flow down and then I'd start to figure out my lyrics from the flow, because people respond to that right away. Sometimes I'd wanna know my exact physical response to a beat without worrying about what I'm gonna rap about.

Devin the Dude

When you develop your flow, even if your subject matter isn't always right there where everybody can understand what it is, or it really doesn't make sense—if your flow is tight, you'll eventually come up with some sort of cool subject matter.

Of course, knowing many different rhythmic techniques helps immensely with this method of starting with the flow, as you have a lot of different rhythmic building blocks to create your flows. Rhythm is also closely linked to enunciation—if you can't say individual syllables clearly, it is very hard to put them precisely in time to the music. For more on enunciation, see chapter 4 of this book, p. 195.

16ths

The most common types of rapped rhythms are created by dividing each bar up into 16 segments—we can call these segments 16ths.

The following diagram illustrates how the main four beats of each bar can be shown along the top of a flow diagram, with each of those four quarters of the bar split into four more parts, to create 16ths:

1				2				3				4			
1	2	3	4	5	6	7	8	9	10	11	12	13	14	15	16

To show how lyrics fit into this structure, here is an example from Spoonie Gee and the Treacherous Three's "The New Rap Language" (01:12) shown here with just the four beats along the top:

1	2	3	4
super scooper,	**par**ty trooper	**man** with all the	**su**per-duper . . .

This song is one of the clearest to demonstrate 16ths with, as the vast majority of the lyrics throughout the song are split into very clear 16th segments, pronounced precisely and exactly on time within each 16th section of the bar.

Here is the same line from the same song, this time showing how the bar and lyrics can be broken down clearly into 16ths:

1				2				3				4			
1	2	3	4	5	6	7	8	9	10	11	12	13	14	15	16
su-	per	scoo-	per,	**par-**	ty	troo-	per	**man**	with	all	the	**su-**	per-	du-	per . . .

When you listen to the song, you can hear the rhythm that the 16ths create, and you can count along with the 16ths as the MCs are rapping (saying, "1, 2, 3, 4, **5**, 6, 7, 8 . . ." etc., as they say each syllable of the lyrics).

Raps based around 16ths rhythms have been around since the early years of hip-hop—as evidenced by the Treacherous Three lyrics above, which are from 1980—and they are still the basis for most rap rhythms today.

Big Daddy Kane

There were great lyricists before us [the MCs from the mid to late '80s]. I don't know if you've heard any of the Kool Moe Dee stuff when he was with the Treacherous Three, but Kool Moe Dee was an incredible MC, early '80s, late '70s. It's like when you listen to Rakim, you can hear a heavy Kool Moe Dee influence.

Crooked I

I learned how to rap listening to old school people—I used to hear old school rappers like Kool Moe Dee and the Treacherous Three, and Busy Bee, and Schoolly D, and Just-Ice. And when I got [a bit older, I also listened to] Boogie Down Productions, and Rakim, Kool G Rap. I just listened to them kinda guys since I was real young, and I kinda picked up a knack for rhyming. I used to memorize their lyrics and spit them as if they were mine [when I first started learning].

Styles Using 16ths

If 16ths are used on a beat that is at a midtempo (medium speed), then it will often make the rapping sound conversational and like everyday speech. This is because when 16ths are rapped over a midtempo beat, it closely mimics the speed at which most people speak—it's not slow like a chant or fast like a speed rap, it's at a conversational pace. This is useful if you want the flow to showcase your content without overshadowing it.

One Be Lo, Binary Star

My favorite MCs are the ones who sound like they're talking to you. Sometimes the rhythm is more dominant than the actual commentary, but I try to write my rhymes in a way where even though it's a specific rhythm or a specific word pattern, that unless you're closely paying attention to it, you don't even really notice it. I leave that for the people who want to study that, but for the people who don't, I just wanna make sure that they're swallowing what I'm saying, as opposed to like, "Oh, man, that rhythm is crazy!"

Using 16ths on a midtempo beat allows rap lyrics to be reasonably sophisticated rhythmically, but not so fast that the content will be hard to decipher. For example, many Nas and Jay-Z songs mostly use rhythms in 16ths over midtempo beats, like this example of a line from Nas's "It Ain't Hard to Tell" (00:38):

1				2				3				4			
1	2	3	4	5	6	7	8	9	10	11	12	13	14	15	16
spar- kle	like	a	dia-	mond,	sneak a			Uz-	i	on	the	is-	land	in	my...

This type of conversational flow really allows Nas's incisive content to take center stage, while still being rhythmically complex and precise.

Brother J, X Clan

I admire Nas when he's poetic—I like when he does like really busting like [on] "One Mic." I wanna hear him do more of that Lauryn Hill, like really talk like a dude who's been there, done that. Talking about, if I ruled the world at this stage this is what I would do, I would build with positivity and with some kind of love for tomorrow's youth for the seeds, for the understanding man. I like to see artists of that kind of writing capability step there.

The speed of a track is usually measured in *beats per minute*, which is shortened to *bpm*. This counts the number of beats that occur in each minute of music. Around 90 to 100 bpm would be considered a midtempo beat—the slower the beat, the more room there is for the syllables in the rap.

Esoteric

"Murder Death Kill" is around 90 beats per minute, so I was able to get more syllables out of each bar. The artist is given more space to create when rhyming at a slower tempo, which is probably the reason people dig East Flatbush Project's "Tried by 12" [instrumental] so much for freestyles . . . it is 88 bpm.

16ths on Faster Beats

The second most common use of 16ths is to rap them over faster beats, which creates a faster rap—this was popular on many classic 1980s hip-hop tracks, such as Big Daddy Kane's "Set It Off," Kool G Rap's "Men at Work," Rakim's "Lyrics of Fury," and the earlier example, Spoonie Gee and the Treacherous Three's "The New Rap Language." Although it is not done as often in more recent hip-hop, it can still be used to good effect.

Big Daddy Kane

Big Pun had a Kool G Rap kind of flow, but it was, like, during a time when no one else was trying to have that faster flow—everybody else was either trying to sound like Jay-Z or Jadakiss. And Pun came with that fast G Rap kind of flow and he won—he was different, he stood out.

With this use of 16ths, the beat will actually determine the speed of the flow—anything upwards of 100 bpm is generally considered a fast beat, and an especially fast beat would be around 120 bpm. This doesn't always mean that the lyrics have to be written to the beat, as sometimes a rap can be written for a midtempo beat and then simply rapped faster over a fast beat later.

Kool G Rap

All my early records I didn't write to the tracks. I don't think I started writing to the tracks until the third album.

Big Daddy Kane

I have faster songs . . . "Warm It Up Kane" and "Set It Off" are the same tempo, they're both 113 [bpm] and "Wrath of Kane" I think is like 120 to 125.

Esoteric

"Daisycutta" is 112 beats per minute, so it gives you less time to squeeze words in, so you adapt to the drums.

Variations with 16ths

The previous examples showed lines that had a syllable on every 16th segment of the bar. However, to create variation and different patterns, certain segments can have no syllables said on them, and certain syllables can be stretched to cover two or more 16ths. Here is another line from Spoonie Gee and the Treacherous Three's "The New Rap Language" (01:19):

1				2				3				4			
1	2	3	4	5	6	7	8	9	10	11	12	13	14	15	16
mon-ey-		mak- ing,		earth			quak- ing	man	who	gets	the	par-	ty	shak- ing.	

The highlighted segment does not have a syllable in it. This breaks up the regular pattern to create variety, so that not every single 16th segment of the bar is occupied by a syllable.

This is an example from Nas's "Represent" (00:20):

1				2				3				4			
1	2	3	4	5	6	7	8	9	10	11	12	13	14	15	16
real	and	an-	y	day	could	be	your	last		in	the	jun-	gle,		get
mur-	dered	on	the	hum-	ble,	guns'	ll	blast		nig-	gas	tum-	ble,		the . . .

Here, most of the 16ths in both bars are filled with individual syllables, except for the highlighted places. In the first bar, the 9th and 10th segments are both taken up with the syllable "last," and the 15th segment is empty. Similarly, in the second bar, the 9th and 10th segments are both covered with one syllable, "blast," and the 15th segment is left empty.

Again, variety is created in the example by altering where the syllables are present and not present, as well as lengthening certain syllables to cover more than one 16th segment. We will see more examples of lengthening certain syllables in chapter 2 (p. 108).

Using 16ths in this way with subtle variations makes it possible to maintain a relatively complex and interesting flow, while still keeping it conversational and easily understandable to the listener. A lot of MCs find this kind of flow ideal because of this balance—this type of flow isn't overly simplistic, and it's not too difficult for the listener to make out the content.

Wordsworth

So hip-hop is a conversation, right, rapping, it's a conversation. When you talk to people on a normal daily basis, you just get your point across. It's about getting your point across as graphic as you can, and as fluent as you can, and as easy as you can so that the listener can feel you. If you're too difficult for the listener to feel you, then you might as well just not write it.

32nds

When it comes to rapping fast, the simplest rhythmical technique is to break the rhythmic units down even further, into 32nds. As there are twice as many of these segments than in 16ths, it requires rapping twice as fast to fit in all the syllables. Therefore it's sometimes known as "double-time" rapping, as the MC is saying double the number of syllables as normal.

Here is a diagram showing how a bar can be broken down into these smaller 32nd segments:

1				2				3				4			
1	2	3	4	5	6	7	8	9	10	11	12	13	14	15	16
1 2	3 4	5 6	7 8	9 10	11 12	13 14	15 16	17 18	19 20	21 22	23 24	25 26	27 28	29 30	31 32

The following is a bar of lyrics from Twista's verse on "Slow Jamz" (02:16) (the flow diagram is split into two parts for this example, to fit it on the page—the first half with the first two main beats is shown first, and then the two final beats are in the second half, underneath the first half):

1				2			
1	2	3	4	5	6	7	8
1	2	3	4	5	6	7	8	9	10	11	12	13	14	15	16
	and	ev-	ry	note	will	be	con-	**troll-**	ing	me	I'm	lov-	ing	the	way

3				4			
9		10		11		12		13		14		15		16	
17	18	19	20	21	22	23	24	25	26	27	28	29	30	31	32
you	be	hold-	ing	me	when I		be	**lis-**	ten-	ing	to	Jo-	de-	ci ...	

As you can see and hear, the syllables are said twice as fast to fit them into the bar, with almost all the 32nds in the bar taken up with individual syllables.

To create this kind of style, it is often best to write the lyrics down on paper, rather than improvising them or writing them in your head, so that you are able to play around more with the individual syllables and where they will go. It can also be helpful to really concentrate on crafting just a few bars at a time, to make sure the lyrics line up correctly with the beat.

Twista

Sometimes the rhythm of a track will allow me to do a certain rap style—when it's like a true Twista type of pattern to the beat and I really gotta get intricate with the words, then I choose to sit down and write it out, because I can play with it more. I like to perfect my lyrics—I don't really like the loose rhymes. I wanted to write intricate patterns and perfect my lyrics, [so I] used to [have] a set process when I first started, of just writing four bars . . . concentrate on four bars at a time.

Sometimes the best beats for rapping fast are slower beats, as they give you more space to rap twice as fast as normal, as mentioned in the first *How to Rap*, p. 124. The slower the beat, the easier it gets to rap twice as fast over it—for example, if a beat is at 50 bpm, you could rap over it really slowly, or you could rap over it as if it were a 100 bpm speed beat, by doubling the speed of the rap.

Esoteric

You can be a little more playful at what are perceived as extremely slow or fast tempos. Some people do not realize that 70 bpm and 140 bpm are the same thing, and the only thing that makes them different is the pace of the hi-hat.

To rap fast enough to fit in 32nds, you need very precise enunciation (see chapter 4, p. 195 for more on enunciation), and only certain MCs are able to do this with the required control. The rhythms often sound almost computerized, as they have to be so fast and so precisely in time with the beat.

Tech N9ne

It's computer rhythm, like, "daga-daga-daga-daga." There's so much to say, all that information, you gotta cram it into a quick line.

Twista

Certain people like myself, Eminem, Busta Rhymes, T.I. . . . certain crews and certain artists like us, we spit rhythms a lot when we rap, so we're holding that tradition strong, so that people don't get too sloppy with their rhymes.

Fast Bursts of Syllables with 32nds

32nds are mostly used in fast rapping styles, though they can also be used to create a fast spurt of rhythm in a regular-speed verse. This is a line from Organized Konfusion's "Bring It On" (00:29):

1	2	3	4
out, spit it out, go a- **head** spit it out, that **itty** bitty style you **up**chuck. Better be-			

In this example, the lyric "itty bitty" is said faster than the rest of the lyrics, in 32nds. It is divided into four syllables in this way— "it," "ty," "bit," "ty," each taking up a 32nd segment of the bar.

MCs such as Pharoahe Monch, of Organized Konfusion, like to add a lot of detailed variation like this in the verses and sometimes even in the choruses.

Pharoahe Monch

Before the world heard [the single "Simon Says"], my friends were like, you cannot just fucking be simple, huh? . . . "Itty-bitty-titty committee, pity the fool that acts shitty in the midst of the calm of the witty." They were like, "It's too complicated for a chorus!" And I was like, I don't care. [They were like], the chorus is too long, you should just keep saying, "Get the fuck up" 21 times!

Adding in a few instances of this technique means that fast sections can be used for variety, without having to adopt this style for every song.

Zumbi, Zion I

I can double time, but it's not really my thing. It's not something I really try to specialize in, even though I can do it and

I've done it before on records. But if I'm gonna do it and [if I think] it might be difficult, I'd practice it enough—I'm not gonna put out anything on the record that's gonna sound like, "Oh, he's really trying to make that happen and it's just not working."

Although 32nds can be used to add a fast rush of syllables to a verse, as in the previous example, these fast sections are not often done using 32nds. This is because triplets, which we will look at next, are normally used to add these fast flourishes.

Triplets

Triplets are used a lot by MCs with advanced flows, as well as on many of the most revered classic hip-hop tracks. They are mostly used to add fast flourishes of rhythms to a flow—varying the speed and creating variety and surprise to keep the listener's attention.

Most commonly, triplets are created by saying *three* syllables within the same amount of time that you would normally say *two* 16ths.

The following diagram shows how triplets look against 16ths. The top line shows the four beats of each bar, the second line shows the bar broken up into 16ths, and the bottom line shows how three syllables can be counted in place of every two syllables in the line of 16ths:

1				2				3				4			
1	2	3	4	5	6	7	8	9	10	11	12	13	14	15	16
1 - 2 - 3			1 - 2 - 3			1 - 2 - 3			1 - 2 - 3			1 - 2 - 3			1 - 2 - 3	1 - 2 - 3	1 - 2 - 3

The shaded numbers show an individual example of this. As you count "1, 2" as 16ths, in the same amount of time you can quickly count "1-2-3" as a triplet.

This can clearly be seen and heard throughout the song "The Originators" (02:17) by the Jaz featuring Jay-Z, as shown at the bottom of the following diagram in part of a line that Jay-Z does:

1				2				3				4			
1	2	3	4	5	6	7	8	9	10	11	12	13	14	15	16
1 - 2 - 3			1 - 2 - 3			1 - 2 - 3			1 - 2 - 3			1 - 2 - 3			1 - 2 - 3			1 - 2 - 3			1 - 2 - 3
Thig-git-a		thig-git-a		thig-git-a		thig-git-a		...							

This is a run of four triplets: a group of three syllables ("thig-git-a") are repeated four times in a row, giving a fast, drumroll sort of sound. This example uses random syllables, though any words or syllables can be used, as long as they are in groups of three syllables and said in the same space where two 16ths would normally be said.

For example, another line from the same song is said entirely in triplets and is made up of words rather than random syllables— "teach-ing-and," "reach-ing-and," "preach-ing-and," "show-ing-and," "flow-ing-and," "grow-ing-and," "blow-ing-the," and "rest-of-the."

If we place the line from Spoonie Gee and the Treacherous Three's example (previously used to show 16ths) next to this line full of triplets, we can see how every group of two 16ths lines up with each triplet:

1		2				3				4			
su- per	scoo- per,	par- ty	troo- per	man with	all	the	su- per	du- per...					
Thig-git-a	thig-git-a	thig-git-a	thig-git-a	thig-git-a	thig-git-a	thig-git-a	thig-git-a...						

Fast Rapping Style with Triplets

The example from the song "The Originators" by the Jaz demonstrates a style in which triplets are used repeatedly to make up most of the lines. This creates a type of fast rapping style, as there will be more syllables in each line than normal with this method. This style was popularized by groups such as Das EFX and Fu-Schnickens in the early 1990s on tracks such as Das EFX's "Mic Checka" and Fu-Schnickens's "What's Up Doc?"

The distinct sound of the triplets makes this a popular technique to use in combination with rhyming fast with 32nds to give variation to a fast rapping style. This style works for some MCs, but not for others, as some MCs feel that they don't sound as good when rapping fast.

Andy Cat, Ugly Duckling

Early on, I remember trying to do a lot more tongue-twisting and really packing in words, because that was the kinda hip thing to do. [The] D.O.C. had a song called "Mind Blowing" and Dres from Black Sheep was really good at that stuff. Ed O.G. had a few lines I really liked, where he was going [fast], and Chip-Fu [of Fu-Schnickens] was really, really good, and was real suitable for that sort of thing. I remember trying to do it a few times and learning eventually that that doesn't work for me, and it doesn't work for our style. But there are a few people who pulled it off and made it work—Busta Rhymes does a bit of it here and there.

Fast Run of Triplets to Break Up a Verse

A common use of triplets is to create a sudden fast section in the middle of an otherwise regular speed verse. Treach's verse on South Central Cartel's "Sowhatusayin" (05:13) does this:

1				2				3				4			
1	2	3	4	5	6	7	8	9	10	11	12	13	14	15	16
T-to-the		R-to-the		E-to-the		A-to-the		C-to-the		H...					

The line "T to the R to the E to the A to the C to the H . . ." is said entirely in triplets—"T-to-the," "R-to-the," "E-to-the," "A-to-the,"

"C-to-the," are each three syllables long, and each is said where two 16th syllables would be said using regular 16th segments.

This line appears at the end of the verse to give it a fast, punchy finish. The rest of the verse varies in speed, while this is a line that uses five triplets in a row to create an impressive flourish.

El Da Sensei

I'll start off kinda slow, but I know that by the time I get to the bottom of this verse, I better have [done something impressive], and it's gotta be set up before you get to the kill. By the time you get to a certain point, I'm looking at it like, "All right, this is kinda plain," so if you can then come [with several triplets, like] "dadada, dadada, dadada" and end it off with [that, then] it's like watching a movie. You know this guy is about to get shot, but you want [it to be done in an impressive way, you want] that person to look at it and say, "Oh, damn," because that's what makes people like you. It depends on how you wanna be perceived as an MC—how much you put that in there.

Single Triplets in a Medium-Paced Flow

To add variety to a conversational flow or a more melodic sing-songy flow, some MCs will drop in a triplet or two every few bars.

This technique can be seen in these lines from Dr. Dre's "Nuthin' but a G Thang" (00:19) featuring Snoop Dogg:

1	2	3	4
			Gim-me-the **mic**rophone
first so I can	**bust** like a	**bub**ble.	**Comp**ton and . . .

The otherwise laid-back and casually rapped flow has individual instances of triplets scattered throughout to keep it interesting and varied.

Similarly, on Jay-Z's *Reasonable Doubt* album, he uses a conversational flow using mostly 16ths, but punctuates this flow with triplets every so often, such as on this line from "Can't Knock the Hustle" (01:21):

1	2	3	4
Fifty	**Gs** to-the-crap	**shoot**er,	**nig**gas can't fade . . .

This method is also used throughout Big L's album, *Lifestylez Ov Da Poor & Dangerous.*

Fredro Starr, Onyx

I might be rhyming at a fast pace with high energy, and then I might rhyme at a slow pace with low energy . . . so I like to just have fun with it, do different things with the beat, try different things, experiment. I think my flow changes on almost every record. I don't like to keep nothing the same.

Opening a Verse or New Line with a Triplet

An effective way to begin a verse or a new line (for example, after a rest or a change in content), is to begin with a triplet before going into a more regular flow, using 16ths. This has the effect of creating momentum and launching into the verse or line, similar to the way that a drummer might do a small drum roll or fill before starting a song or before a new section of a song.

Here is an example from Organized Konfusion's "Why" (00:32), in which a triplet is used before the first main bar of the verse to help spring forward into the verse:

1	2	3	4
			You're sneak-ing-a-
round like a	**sneak**er, baby,	**what's** the beeper	**for?**

The triplet, "sneak-ing-a-" is used as a type of roll to bring us into the first full line of the verse.

Several Das EFX tracks make great use of this technique to bring in a lot of energy right at the beginning of the track. Here's an example from their song, "They Want EFX" (00:08):

1	2	3	4
		Bum stig-ged-y	**bum** stig-ged-y
bum, hon, I	**got** that old pa-	**rrrum**-pa-pum-	**pum** but I can . . .

"Stig-ged-y" is said twice using fast triplets before the first main bar of the lyrics come in, similar to a drum roll that a drummer might do before the start of a song.

Adding in fast triplets like this can really help to keep the flow varied and unpredictable, to keep the listener's attention.

Dray, Das EFX

We did [keep the flows changing and unpredictable] consciously and purposely. That's one of the conscious things I did. When I listened to other rappers I used to hate just hearing the same monotonous flow all the way through the song. It might have been saying good shit, but they lost me halfway through because their flow was just so boring. Like vanilla, black and white, it wasn't nothing colorful—splash. So when I'm gonna write a verse I'm always gonna mix it up for the listener, especially if you're an MC.

Triplets with Repeating Phrases

Triplets are often used in ragga-influenced styles, in which a phrase will be repeated quickly with triplets.

Tajai, Souls of Mischief

You listen to a lot of dancehall MCs and [music] like that, and they'll out-rap regular rappers a thousand to one. But they're in other genres—they're not even in the "rap" genre, even though they're rapping.

The group Fu-Schnickens's song "True Fuschnick" (01:15) has the word "bubbling" said in triplets (as "bub-ble-ing") and repeated many times:

1	2	3	4
Bub-ble-ing bub-ble-ing **bub**-ble-ing bub-ble-ing **bub**-ble-ing bub-ble-ing **bub**-ble-ing bub-ble-ing			
bub-ble-ing bub-ble-ing **bub**-ble-ing bub-ble-ing **bub**-ble-ing until they're **boiled**, so . . .			

Kris Kross's "Jump" (02:11) has a whole section that revolves around the use of this technique, in which "migity" is repeated several times as triplets, as shown in the lines below:

1	2	3	4
Mig-it-y mig-it-y	**mig**-it-y mig-it-y	**Mack** Daddy,	the
Mig-it-y mig-it-y	**mig**-it-y mig-it-y	**Mack**.	

Similarly, KRS-One repeats the phrase "off-i-cer" as triplets in the song "Sound of Da Police" (01:39) (the rhythmic technique is also cleverly tied in with the content to show the similarities between "overseers" and "officers," something which is looked at in chapter 2, p. 119):

1	2	3	4
	over- **se**er,	**off**-i-cer, **off**-i-cer, off-i-cer,	**off**icer . . .

These kinds of rapid-fire bursts of syllables are usually used to show the dexterity of the MC, so they can be hard for listeners to imitate and rap along to themselves. However, fans still often appreciate the musicality and difficulty of the techniques, even if it makes it harder for them to sing along with the lyrics.

Twista

Artists like Bone Thugs-N-Harmony, artists like myself, people can't really rap along with all the lyrics, but they vibe with the song, [because] your lyrics to a beat is still really a *sound* moving in unison with the beat.

Triplets Broken Up with Extra Syllables

Most of the examples of triplets we have looked at so far have occurred directly after one another, in a fast run of triplets. However, they can also be broken up with other syllables to spread them out and create a different effect.

If we look at this line from the chorus of Brotha Lynch Hung's "Season of Da Sicc" (01:20), the repeated phrase is "wick-ed-I":

1	2	3	4
Wick-ed-I come,	wick-ed-**I** come, wick-ed-I	**eat** you up sty-	**lee**, if I don't . . .

The triplets are spread out so that the word "come" separates them and adds to the variety of the rhythm. The first syllable of the first triplet falls on the beat, as "**wick**-ed-I," but then the last syllable of the next triplet falls on the beat, "wick-ed-**I**," and the third triplet in the line falls in between beats, "wick-ed-I."

Each triplet still takes up the same amount of time as two 16ths, but they are placed in more unusual positions than if they were to be said directly after each other, as with previous examples.

The same rhythmic technique, using triplets broken up with extra syllables, is used at the end of Spice 1's "Trigga Gots No Heart" (02:44), as shown in this line:

1	2	3	4
kill-a-man say,	kill-a-**man** say, kill-a-man	**kill**-a-man with me	**glock**, glock.

Organized Konfusion's "The Extinction Agenda" (02:32) has an interesting use of a repeated phrase, "check it again," in which "check-it-a-" is a triplet, and an extra syllable, "-gain" is used to add variety between the triplets:

1	2	3	4
	Check-it-a-**gain**,	**check**-it-a- gain,	**check**-it-a- gain . . .

Again, shifting the triplets into different positions in this way creates complex and interesting rhythmic patterns. Of course, with any of the above rhythms, there doesn't have to be a repeated phrase, the rhythm could be done using any words, though this rhythm just happens to be closely linked to a repeated phrase.

This is the type of technique in which content is often sacrificed in favor of flow—words are frequently chosen simply because they sound good when placed in a particular rhythm. This can work because the flow can be an entertaining thing in itself, without the need for content.

Thes One, People Under the Stairs

See, I don't know if content is necessary ever, maybe, because some of my favorite rhymes of all time have had nothing to do with anything. It's tough to say, man, I don't think people can be a stickler for content—there's too many classics that don't have any content to them at all.

Crooked I

MCing is moving forward—the other day, I had some guys come to my studio from Japan and they couldn't speak any English, but I loved the way they were rapping. Any time you got people who can come all the way out here from Japan and not even be able to communicate through English, but communicate through music, [then] you gotta believe it's moving forward.

Triplets on Slower Beats

Triplets have a different feel over slower beats—the triplets are either slowed down, because the beat is slower, or they are doubled up, to get twice as many of them in.

Spice 1's "Dumpin' Em in Ditches" (01:41 on the album version of the song) includes the line "Jealous niggas be wanting to gat me because they can't rise," which contains the three triplets below:

1				2				3				4			
1	2	3	4	5	6	7	8	9	10	11	12	**13**	14	15	16
Nig-gas-be	want-ing-to	**gat**-me-be-	cause . . .												

Because it is over a slower beat than normal, the triplets create a more staggered and "swung" feel, as opposed to when they are repeated quickly over a more mid-tempo beat, as in earlier examples. This technique is also used a lot by Bone Thugs-N-Harmony, who tend to rap over slower-tempo beats and so often use triplets in this way to add variety.

In this technique, the speed of the beat can determine the sound of the flow—if the beat is a slower speed, it will mean that you can space out triplets in this way and get this particular sounding flow.

Rampage, Flipmode Squad

It depends on if the beat is moving fast, that's what type of flow I'll come with. I don't want to never clash against the beat, I just want to make sure I put on something just right that's gonna go aside with the beat, to make the beat sound official.

R.A. the Rugged Man

I like doing that a lot too, writing to beats. When you're trying to do like an ill flow, you're taking the bassline and the drum and the kick and riding that shit like you never could do just writing in your notebook. For flows, it's me sitting in my room with the radio, bumping beats all day, boom boom, all week, all month, all year. Every time I work on my album, when I'm rhyming on my album, shit that I'm gonna have to listen to and perform for goddamn 20 years and more after it's done, I'll always just write to the real beat that I'm rhyming to.

Triplets over Four 16ths

A variation on doing a regular triplet is done by rapping a group of three syllables in place of *four* 16ths, instead of two 16ths.

This is how it looks in a diagram in which the top line shows the four beats in a bar, the second line are 16ths, and the bottom line are triplets that are said over the course of four 16ths:

1				2				3				4			
1	2	3	4	5	6	7	8	9	10	11	12	13	14	15	16
1	-	2	-	3	1	-	2	-	3	1	-	2	-	3	1 - 2 - 3

This gives the "swung" feel of triplets, but spread further over the beat so the triplets are slower. It sounds similar to when regular triplets are rapped over a slower beat, as in an earlier example.

Here is an example from Chubb Rock's "Ya Bad Chubbs" (01:11), which uses this technique:

1		2		3		4		
mop - up - the	**slop** - and - then	**go** - to - the	**top** - I - am
not - Ro - bo	**Cop**, I'm	**Chubb** Rock.	

This uses several of these triplets in a row, each spread over four 16ths, with the first triplet highlighted. The triplets are, "mop-up-the," "slop-and-then," "go-to-the," "top-I-am," and "not-Ro-bo."

Saying three syllables as triplets in this way, spread over four 16ths, sounds different to when three normal 16ths are rapped. This is because with the triplet technique, the three syllables are spread more evenly, giving the "swung" feel to them.

R.A. the Rugged Man

A lot of times, there's a certain bass underneath or a certain swing that a sample gives or something that you're almost harmonizing your vocals with the track sometimes, and sometimes when you put it to another beat it doesn't have the same swing.

Unconventional Placement of Triplets

Normally, triplets come one after the other and fit in the bars of music in a standard way, such as in many of the previous examples. As we've seen, they also can be separated by extra syllables placed in between them, which makes them fall in less regular places. Additionally, they can also be placed in an arrangement in which they are broken up with slight pauses rather than extra syllables.

Here is an example from Dr. Dre and Snoop Dogg's "187um" (01:30):

1	2	3	4
Get-a-way	**set**-a-way	get-a-**way**,	Snoop's got a **gun**.

Here, "get-a-way" and "set-a-way" fall in obvious places, one directly after the other, but the second "get-a-way" doesn't fall directly after "set-a-way," it falls slightly later so that "-way" falls on the 3 beat. In this instance, there isn't an extra syllable to move them further apart, there is just a slight pause between "set-a-way" and the second "get-a-way."

Playing around with the placement of triplets, rather than doing them in one fast run with one directly after the other, is a good way to create variation.

T3, Slum Village

My background is more on the [rhythmic] style, [rather than focused on content], so I was more into certain albums. Back in the '90s, there was a lot of rappers [doing a lot of different rhythms] like the Rumpletilskinz did a lot of lyrical styles and Leaders of the New School. Back then they did a lot of [flow] techniques that inspired me and my whole style.

Note on triplets: A "triplet" in rapping also refers to slightly unevenly placed groups of three syllables over two 16ths: either two 32nds and a 16th, or a 16th and two 32nds, as well as the regular use of the term "triplet," in which the syllables are evenly spaced over the two 16ths. When they are rapped quickly, as they normally are, they all sound the same.

Making sure the three syllables are evenly spaced only makes a difference in how they sound when they are done over a slower beat or when they are done over four 16ths, where they are rapped more slowly and so have to be more evenly spaced to have a "swung" feel.

Flams

In drumming and percussion, a flam is a technique in which you have a soft drum hit immediately followed by a louder hit, to make a "ta-*dum*" sound. The same technique is used in rapping with syllables instead of drum hits.

Evidence, Dilated Peoples

Sometimes, the beat dictates [the flow and gives you rhythmic techniques]—if the drum is going "ka-*kah*, ka-*kah*," it'd be nice to [rap along] with it. The drum usually is the basis of everything, [and it gives you techniques to use].

When rapping flams, the syllables are said close enough together to make one continuous sound out of the two syllables—because of this, they are shown joined together with a dash, as in "the-dirt."

An obvious example of this is throughout DMX's "Who We Be" (00:48), in which the whole flow revolves around flams. Here is an example from the song:

1	2	3	4	
				the-
hurt	the-**pain**	the-**dirt**	the-**rain**	the-
jerk	the-**fame**	the-**work**	the-**game** . . .	

As you can see and hear, the lyrics in the example are all made up of a soft syllable followed by a syllable with more emphasis, as in "the-**pain**," "the-**dirt**," and so on. All the groups of two syllables in this example are that type of flam.

Alternatively, a flam can be created by the opposite combination, by a strong hit followed by a softer hit, a "*dum*-ta" sound. Here is an example of this from Lucas's "The Muted Trumpet" (00:41):

1	2	3	4
When-I	**take**-a	**hard**-look	**at** my boys . . .

Here, the examples of "**when**-I," "**take**-a," and "**hard**-look" are all flams that work in this way—as an emphasized syllable quickly followed by a softer syllable.

Some tracks use both versions of flams, as in this example from Dr. Dre's "Deeez Nuuuts" (02:01):

1	2	3	4
	. . . damn, I **ripped**-up	flipped-**up**, and	**skipped**-up, on . . .

The first flam, "**ripped**-up," is the "*dum*-ta" type, followed by "flipped-**up**," which is the "ta-*dum*" type, and then "**skipped**-up" which is back to the "*dum*-ta" type.

Using flams is a great way to deliver short words and phrases in quick bursts, as it naturally breaks up the lyrics into smaller rhythmic pieces.

Del the Funky Homosapien

I'm trying to reach that essence—saying what you mean quick, but with flavor. That's how they rapped in the '70s, and that is my goal, like, "Keep it solid and polished." Little phrases, like pimps talk like that. They always got little lines they bust out. The thing is, it's entertaining and it gets you into what they saying. It's influential. Catchy, even.

Andy Cat, Ugly Duckling

Your rhythmic ability—some people are extremely rhythm-oriented, and understand rhythm to such a degree [that] they're really creative with ideas and can break stuff down into really small bits, and word schemes.

Particularly fast MCs, such as Fu-Schnickens on "Heavenly Father" (01:03), can do flams in which there are two very fast softer syllables followed by a stressed syllable to create a flam that sounds like "ta-ta-*dum*" (this is also known as a "ruff" or a "drag" in drumming):

1	2	3	4
			To-the-
Poc,	on-my-**right**,	and-the-**Moc**,	on-my-**left** . . .

Each of the beats in the example above have one of these flams landing on them, such as "on-my-**right**" falling on the 2 beat of the bar.

Alternatively, instead of a "ta-ta-*dum*" flam, there is a "*dum*-ta-ta" flam, in which there is a strong syllable followed quickly by two softer syllables. An example of this is on Brotha Lynch Hung's "Dead Man Walking" (01:19):

1	2	3	4
give-it-up, then I'm	**in**-the-cut, five	tri**ple oh, double oh,**	**Moss**berg pump . . .

The lyrics "**give**-it-up" and "**in**-the-cut" are examples of this kind of "*dum*-ta-ta" flam.

Both the "*dum*-ta-ta" flam and the "ta-ta-*dum*" flam can be said as a triplet (which are explained previously) if they are said at the same speed as a triplet (in which three syllables are said in the same space as two regular 16th syllables) or they can just be said very quickly to make a single sound out of three syllables being said fast and run into each other.

On Snoop Dogg's "Doggy Dogg World" (00:40), he uses both the "*dum*-ta-ta" flam and the "ta-ta-*dum*" flam in a single line:

1	2	3	4
So put your	**gun**-a-way,	run-a-**way**, 'cause I'm	**back**. Why?

"**Gun**-a-way" is a "*dum*-ta-ta" flam, followed by "run-a-**way**" which is a "ta-ta-*dum*" flam.

Tajai, Souls of Mischief

[If] I'm thinking of it in pieces, if you break it down into pieces, it's more intricate, because I'm thinking of it bit by bit and then connecting it.

The Lady of Rage

You definitely want to change your flow and change your rhythm and change all of that, to keep people guessing or to make it interesting.

One Syllable on Each Beat

A good way to break up a flow, particularly to slow down a rapid-fire flow for a moment, is to place just a single syllable on each beat of a bar.

On Snoop Dogg's "Pump, Pump" (01:36), the following lyrics are spaced out so that there is mainly just one syllable on each beat of the bar:

1	2	3	4
When,	then,	send, some	gin . . .

By abruptly switching to just placing single syllables on the beat, it slows down the flow and provides a change of pace. Snoop Dogg uses the same technique at the beginning of his first verse on Dr. Dre's "Nuthin' but a G Thang."

An early example of this technique is on Sugarhill Gang's "Rapper's Delight" (02:01), in which it is also used to split up two words across a whole bar:

1	2	3	4
ho-	tel,	mo-	tel . . .

This again has the effect of breaking up the rest of the flow by slowing it down, as well as putting more focus onto these particular words.

This technique is sometimes used to repeat one particular word, to emphasize it. This is heard on Fu-Schnickens's "La Schmoove" (00:26):

1	2	3	4
rocking	beats	beats	beats . . .

This technique means you use fewer words for the particular bars that you use it over, but sometimes this can be an advantage, as you are forced to choose the words more carefully.

Lateef, Latyrx

[In a song,] it's a finite amount of time, so you can't always be as descriptive or as long winded as you want. It really is an art form where "brevity is the soul of wit," the more you can say with the least amount of words. I used to be like, "Oh, man, how many words can I fit into these four bars?" and now it's like, "How few words can I use to really convey this heavy, incredibly descriptive topic?" So you think of people who have done it well, like Bob Marley, "concrete jungle," I know exactly what you're talking about in two words, four syllables and I know exactly what you're talking about.

Along with rests, this technique is also good for providing places to breathe within a track—slowing down the flow allows the MC to take a deep breath in between the words, so they can then continue with a faster-paced flow.

Big Daddy Kane

I might slow up the flow for two bars so I can take a deep breath, so that it can run through [smoothly]. I've seen a lot of people try to do fast songs and then when they perform live they can't even say their own lyrics—so I try to make it where I have those spots where I can catch a breath.

Sliding Off the Beat (Lazy Tails)

The following technique is used often by a lot of West Coast MCs—it is a very distinct element of their style, particularly in early 1990s West Coast gangsta rap.

Shock G, Digital Underground

When I scrutinize my memory about it, it does seem to have evolved on the West Coast, I can't think of a single pre-West song that has that.

In this technique, the rapping is squarely in time to the beat, apart from certain syllables or words that are said so that they slide off the beat. This adds variation to the flow and gives it a laid-back feel. Often the first letter is said slightly after the beat and the whole syllable or word is drawn out, for effect.

It is a type of syncopation, as described in the first *How to Rap* (pp. 256–257), except rather than the entire flow being placed slightly behind or in front of the beat, this is used only on particular syllables. It is also a different technique from placing syllables clearly and obviously off beat, which is looked at later in this chapter (p. 46).

Here is an example of two bars from Kam's "Still Got Love 4 'Um" (01:44):

1	2	3	4
see how they was	**liv**ing, how their	**life** was	**look**ing,
got their	**sis**ters and	**ate** their momma's	cccooking.

In these lines, the rapping is on the beat, until the final rhyme on the 4 beat of the couplet. Instead of "cooking" lying perfectly in time to the beat (with "cook" falling directly on the 4 beat, as in "**cook**ing") the word is slid off the beat, slightly extending the first letter, the "c" sound. This makes the line sound more laid-back and gives it a certain relaxed character.

Another example is from the very beginning of Ice Cube's "Color Blind" (00:01):

1	2	3	4
Here's another	day at the	ssstoplight.	I'm
looking in my	**mir**ror so I can	sssee who can	sssee me.

He uses the technique several times in these opening lyrics. In the first bar he puts "day" slightly off beat as well as sliding "stoplight" off the beat while extending the "s" sound. In the second bar, he extends the "s" both times he says "see," and slides them both after the beat.

Shock G has referred to this technique as "lazy tails"—a very fitting description, as they usually occur toward the end of a sentence and the "tail" hangs "lazily" behind the beat rather than directly on it.

Shock G, Digital Underground

The MCs around me in [Digital Underground] were on that [technique] in 1990 already—2Pac and Pee Wee especially. Check out how Pee Wee lags the middle parts of his opening two sentences, right out the gate on [Gold Money]'s "Youngblood," [although I'm] not saying they created it of course. I remember they were both big on Scarface and MC Ren, who used to flip like that sometimes, and we all were on Ice Cube and Eazy-E. I think when it really started to creep into my psyche was when Numskull and Yukmouth [of the Luniz] started coming around during work on the first Luniz album. The Luniz were notorious for laying behind that beat. The "I Got 5 on It" single is laced with those lazy tails!

An example in which the technique is not used in the context of a relaxed West Coast flow is in these lyrics by Fu-Schnickens on "True Fuschnick" (00:39). Instead, it is used during a rapid-fire flow, sliding the word "flow" after the 4 beat:

1	2	3	4
Uh oh, better get	**Maa**co, chocolate	**Chip**'s about to	ffffllow.

Sliding the Next Syllable onto the Beat

Sometimes the lyrics are slid far enough off the beat that not only is the syllable that would normally fall on the beat slid off that beat, but the syllable before it ends up landing on the beat instead. For example, here is part of the chorus of Cypress Hill's "How I Could Just Kill a Man" (00:49):

1	2	3	4
Here is	something you	can't un-	dersssttttaaaaand . . .

The line is set up so you might expect the syllable "-stand" to fall on the 4 beat. Instead it is slid off the beat to where the previous syllable "-der" falls on the beat instead.

This line from the beginning of Dr. Dre and Snoop Dogg's "Nuthin' but a G Thang" (00:10) uses a similar technique:

1	2	3	4
One,	two,	three, and to	the four . . .

Here, you would expect "four" to land squarely on the 4 beat, but it slides off so that "the" lands on the 4 beat instead.

Sliding off the beat in these ways can give your flow a very relaxed, chilled feel, and this suits a lot of MCs' personalities. MCs often find it fun to alter the rhythm with techniques such as this, playing around with the flow to give it more character.

Lateef, Latyrx

The thing about a flow is it should be an extension of the personality of the person. So if the personality is strong and it comes across in the flow, then a lot of times you're gonna be able to pull people into your subject matter.

Del the Funky Homosapien

Rhythmically, how you swing, and playing something funky or with a groove, is [like] you're playing with it. It would bore you to just sit up there and [rap] it normally, just straight and stiff, so to entertain your own self, you like doing other shit with it. Think of it like [this]: Somebody that's a pro at [the video game] *Street Fighter* is not gonna want to sit on *Street Fighter* and just play stiff, normally—they're gonna want to entertain themselves by doing [lots of techniques]! They're gonna floss with it a little bit. So anybody that's looking at them playing, it's damn near like watching a cartoon, they're so good.

Rolled *R*s

Although not used that extensively, doing a rolled *r* sound is a good way to add another rhythmic element to the flow. It produces a very fast rolling sound, like a high-speed drum roll. It is limited, however, because words can't be placed into it—it is essentially just a rhythmic sound effect.

One of the most famous uses is in Fat Boys' "Stick 'Em" with the line "Brrrrr, stick 'em." This phrase is extended into "Brrrrr, stick 'em, ha-ha-ha, stick 'em" on Mad Kap's "Da Whole Kit and Kaboodle" and Fu-Schnickens's "What's Up Doc?" as well as used as part of the chorus of Coolio's "Hit 'Em."

Here is an example from Das EFX's "They Want EFX" (00:09) in which we can see a rolled *r* added within a line:

1	2	3	4
bum, hon, I	**got** that old pa-	**rrrum**-pa-pum	**pum** but I can

Jay-Z ties the rolling *r* effect into part of the content of the track, "Can't Get with That" (02:24):

1	2	3	4
So I	**bought** a money ma-	**chine** and	**it** goes, a-
tack tick, drrrrrrrrrrrrr-	**rack** tick, drrrrrrrrrrrrr-	**rack** tick tick tick	**tick** doe.

The highlighted parts show where a long rolling *r* is placed within the lyrics to mimic a money-counting machine.

Lateef, Latyrx

If you think about somebody like Jay-Z, he raps about different shit sometimes, but a lot of times he raps about similar subject matter and it always sounds new and fresh and it's because his flow is strong enough that it's going to pull you into his subject matter. And he's clever enough and charismatic enough that you're going to be entertained by it—the way he says it, it seems new, even if it's a re-tread of subject matter.

Rests

As described in the first *How to Rap* (p. 73), rests occur when an MC pauses on the 1, 2, 3, or 4 beat of a bar.

These are a lot more prominent than just missing a syllable on the offbeats, which was shown with 16ths, because with rests, you hear the beat in the music clearly, as there are no lyrics over it. Rests are often added to create more rhythmic variety and to structure a verse. Here are several ways that rests can be used to do this, which were not covered in the first *How to Rap*.

Rests on the I Beat (Punch-Line Technique)

One of the most popular uses of rests is to rest on the 1 beat of the bar. In Slick Rick's "Lick the Balls" (00:24), he puts rests on a lot of the 1 beats, giving the track a very distinct flow:

1	2	3	4
Around this	**part** of town with	**di**amonds and your	**girl** in fur.
"I'm trying to	**enter** in this	**rap** contest you're	**ha**ving, sir."

In both these lines, the 1 beat has a rest on it, as is highlighted in the diagram.

A very popular use of this technique combines using couplets, in which the rhyme scheme joins two bars together (*How to Rap*, p. 99), with using a hard-hitting or humorous punch line on the second bar of the couplet, and putting a rest on the first 1 beat of the couplet. This can be seen in Eminem's "My Name Is" (00:34):

1	2	3	4
My brain's	**dead** weight, I'm	**try**ing to get my	**head** straight, but I
can't figure	**out** which	**Spice** Girl I wanna im-	**preg**nate.
And Dr.	**Dre** said . . .		

There is a rest on the first 1 beat, then two bars are joined by the rhyme of "head straight" in the first bar and "pregnate" in the second bar. The second bar also contains a punch line ("Can't figure out which Spice Girl I wanna impregnate") and it is followed by another rest on the 1 in the bar after the couplet has ended. This pattern repeats in the song, with a bar with a rest on the 1 beat, then a bar with no rest but with a punch line.

The rest after the punch line gives the punch line more emphasis as there is a pause after it to let it sink in with the listener, which is why this technique is very popular with MCs who use a lot of punch lines. It also naturally divides the content—each couplet is separated by a rest on the 1 beat.

Evidence, Dilated Peoples

If I know I'm going to come in after the beat sometimes I'll write ". . ." and then start my flow, start writing. So I know to miss the 1 [beat]—don't hit the kick drum right there, wait till after it.

Leaving a rest on the 1 beat of every other bar is used so often because it's one of the strongest ways that the flow can support the content—this pattern helps structure the content and makes the content a lot more powerful by emphasizing the witty punch lines on every other bar of the song.

Masta Ace

Both [the content and the flow used together] are equally important, and I tend to try to incorporate both into whatever I'm doing. There'll be moments where it's all about the flow and the wordplay and how it bounces through the track, and then there's other points where I wanna hit you with an impact line or make a profound statement in a line, or hit you with a metaphor or a punch line that you weren't expecting. So I really do try to use both in my writing and I think both are equally important, and I think the best MCs are the ones that are able to incorporate both. I think Jay-Z's a really, really good example of a guy who incorporates punch lines, and incredible flow, and wordplay, cleverness—all those things come into play and they're all equally important. The best guys, they put them all together.

Rest on the 2 Beat (Short Opening Statement Technique)

A common way of starting a verse in the late 1980s, which is occasionally still used in more recent hip-hop, is to say a word or short phrase as an opening "statement" on the 1 beat, followed by a rest on the 2 beat, before going into the rest of the lyrics on the 3 beat.

This really emphasizes the opening short word or phrase, as it's said loudly on the first beat and then left to sink in for a moment, as there is a rest on the 2 beat. Public Enemy does this on a number of tracks, such as "Bring the Noise" (00:15):

1	2	3	4
Bass!	How	low can you	go?

The strongly emphasized word is "bass," which is then followed by a rest on the 2 beat, before the lyrics continue. Another Public Enemy track that does this is "Don't Believe the Hype" (00:12):

1	2	3	4
Back!		Caught you **look**ing for the	**same** thing.

Other Public Enemy tracks that use the technique include "Rebel Without a Pause," "Night of the Living Baseheads," and "Brothers Gonna Work It Out."

A track that uses more than just one word to open the song in this way is Eric B. & Rakim's "In the Ghetto" (00:38), which begins:

1	2	3	4
			Planet
Earth		was my **place** of	**birth**, born to . . .

Here, the opening phrase is "Planet Earth," in which "Earth" falls on the 1 beat and then there is a rest on the 2 beat. Again, this emphasizes the first phrase so that it becomes a strong opening statement.

Multiple Rests

Putting several rests in a short space of time gives an interesting stop-start effect to the rhythm. This is used on Organized Konfusion's "Black Sunday" (00:51) when a single syllable is used to accent the offbeat by surrounding it with rests:

1	2	3	4
ass in the	**fu**ture,	then	

There is a rest placed on the 3 beat of the bar, followed by the word "then" on the offbeat of the 3, then another rest placed on the 4 beat.

Another track with interesting rest placements is the Lady of Rage's "Get with Da Wickedness" (00:08):

1	2	3	4
Ready to	do damage	but just a	little bit
slower to	let you know Rage	is that lyri-	cal flow . . .

Here, two rests occur close together, on the 3 beat of the first bar and then on the 1 beat of the second bar.

Tech N9ne

I put commas [for multiple rests]. Like if I say, "I just want to stop," I'll put a comma after that and then I'm gonna come back in [with the rest of the lyrics].

Dividing Content and Rhyme Schemes with Rests

A good way to divide up the content and rhyme schemes is with rests. As we've seen previously, a series of couplets can each start with a rest on the 1 beat—this means that there is a rest in between each couplet, dividing the content up into two bar segments.

This doesn't have to be done just on the 1 beat. You could divide a verse at any point by simply placing a rest before you start a sentence or a new rhyme scheme, and then placing a rest after it ends, no matter where that happens to be in the bars of music.

You can also divide as much or as little as you like with rests—you could have very short half-bar-long sentences, each separated with a rest, or you could divide a 16-bar verse into two parts by putting a rest on the eighth or ninth bar to signal a divide in the content and/or rhyme schemes.

As with all uses of rests, using a diagram or other notational system is useful, so that you can keep track of where the rests are meant to go.

Shock G, Digital Underground

If I need to remind myself that the next sentence starts earlier or later than the "1" of the beat, I write it further to the left or right in relation to where all the rest of the sentences started.

Like . . .
. . . . . . this.

Big Daddy Kane

If someone else read [my lyrics from the paper I wrote it on],
it may not make no sense, because you'd see a comma where
it doesn't go, but I would understand it—I'd put a comma
there [for a rest].

Interrupting Sentences with Rests

Often, the content of the rap is broken up with rests in interesting
ways. We looked at how rests can be used to divide the content
into contained sections, but they can also be used to give unexpected pauses *within* sentences.

One way of doing this is to start a sentence before the first bar,
then put a rest on the 1 beat, and then continue the sentence,
which places a rest within the beginning of a sentence. This
technique is used by Big Daddy Kane on Prince Paul's "Macula's
Theory" (00:58):

1	2	3	4	
				Mister
spectacu-	lar better	known as Macu-	la . . .	

Here, the line "Mister spectacular . . ." is broken up by saying "mister" on the previous bar, then putting a rest on the 1 beat of the next
bar, then continuing the line with "spectacular, better known . . ."

This lyric from Brotha Lynch Hung's "Season of Da Sicc" (00:26)
shows a rest in the middle of a sentence:

1	2	3	4	
fuck a Smith and	Wesson, I got my		nine at my	chest and I got my . . .

The rest on the 3 beat of the bar, as highlighted, divides the sentence in two.

In this next example from Queen Latifah's "Inside Out" (00:55), the sentence is interrupted on the 1 beat of the bar and then on the 4 beat of the bar:

1	2	3	4	
				... while I
rhyme to the **rhy**thm and		**keep** it blowing		out, so ...

This adds a lot of variation to that particular sentence by placing multiple rests within it.

By interrupting and varying the actual phrasing of the content with the rhythm and where you pause, you can add emphasis and character to what you're saying in many different places within the song—this is another way in which the flow can continually enhance the meaning of the lyrics.

MC Shan

The subject matter *and* the flow, they go hand in hand. If you can have a nice ill flow, something that's crazy that people will listen to, instead of just listening to the beat and then when the hook come on, start singing. The hardest part is to get people to listen to what you're talking about. If you can do that and make it interesting at the same time, now that's a complication.

Rest in the Middle of a Word

Not only can a rest be used to break up sentences, but it can also be used to break up individual words, by being placed in the middle of a word, splitting it up. This is seen in the following line from Das EFX's "Mic Checka" (00:17):

1	2	3	4
miggedy make the	**Won**der Twins	**de**acti-	vate. It's . . .

The word "deactivate" starts on the 3 beat with "deacti-," then there is a rest on the 4 beat, followed by the last part of the word, "-vate," falling after the rest. This can be used to make words sound more interesting, as the listener hears the first part of the word but is left guessing until the second part of the word comes in after the rest.

More than One Rest in a Row

You can rest on several beats, with no syllables said in between, to create a particularly long pause. This is done on Organized Konfusion's "Let's Organize" (01:16):

1	2	3	4
back off, I	**jack** off on	**wack** M-	**Cs** in the vi-
cinity.		Nigga,	**please**, I make them . . .

The highlighted segments show where there is a rest on the 2 beat of the second bar, immediately followed by a rest on the 3 beat of the same bar. This has the effect of a longer than normal pause in the lyrics.

Several rests in a row are used repeatedly on A Tribe Called Quest's "Bonita Applebum" (00:56):

1	2	3	4
			Hey,
being with	**you** is a	**top** pri-	**or**ity.
Ain't no	**need** to	**ques**tion the au-	**thor**ity.

This technique gives the song a more sing-songy feel, as there are relatively few lyrics for a hip-hop song—the number of syllables in the song is closer to a regular pop or rock song.

Sometimes, using an unusual pattern like this can be a great way to bring things out of the musical backing or get your content across to the listener. A unique or stripped-down approach can sometimes be as effective as, or more effective than, an obvious display of technical skill with the flow.

Andy Cat, Ugly Duckling

In our group, we concentrate a lot on the production and musical sound and a lot of the times the lyrics are more a means of getting across the music or theme that we hear in the music. So it's a lot different approach than "I'm just gonna be dopest MC" or kick the greatest verse ever, we're more focused on propelling the music. Groups like A Tribe Called Quest, to me, where Q-Tip was the greatest at that [and] Guru [of Gang Starr] was really good, too, because if you read a Q-Tip verse or a Guru verse and just read the lyrics, you might not be that impressed, but if you hear it along with the track, it really made the track soothing or more powerful, or connects with the listener—that's how I felt. Say something like "Bonita Applebum," it's a weird [flow], it's very mellow, very laid-back, which to me is a genius approach to that track. I'd have never thought to do that, to rap every other line and very cool and kinda seductive, with his voice, but it was a clever way of presenting that track and to me making it probably the most seductive hip-hop song ever, in the way that it's really cool. I think I'm more drawn to people who are very clever in getting something across, which didn't really develop until the late '80s and early '90s. I started enjoying the Native Tongues groups and like I said, Gang Starr, where production came to the forefront and the raps and the songwriting were a means of getting a dope track to sound even better.

Punctuating the Offbeat

In order to punctuate the offbeat, to make it sound punchy and stand out, syllables (or a syllable) have to be said on the offbeat and surrounded by rests and/or slight pauses. If there is no pause on either side, then you don't get the punchy sound of the offbeat being punctuated, because the words simply flow across the offbeat in a continuous stream.

To make the offbeat syllables stand out very clearly, rests can be placed before and after them. However, it is also possible to use just one rest or to use no rests, as we will see. A lot of MCs have specific notation they have come up with to note down these types of elements.

Crooked I

It's kind of like writing music. I have little symbols I use when I write, and that lets me know that I have to emphasize this word or I have to stretch that word out or I have to pause before this word comes in.

Rests Before and After the Offbeat Syllables

The easiest way to punctuate the offbeat is to place rests before and after the offbeat syllables. This creates obvious pauses before and after the syllables.

Here is an example from 2Pac's "Dear Mama" (01:00):

1	2	3	4
You al-	**ways** was a	**black** queen,	Mama.
I	finally under-	**stand** for a	**wom**an it ain't . . .

In the first bar of the example, there is a rest on the 4 beat, followed by "Mama" punctuating the offbeat, followed by a rest on the 1 beat of the second bar. The offbeat word, "Mama," is therefore particularly emphasized because it's surrounded by rests.

A Rest Before the Offbeat Syllables

A very common way to emphasize the offbeat syllables is to have a rest before them, but not after them—there is plenty of room before the offbeat syllables, due to the rest, to make it clear that the offbeat is being punctuated.

Here is an example from Das EFX's "Mic Checka" (00:15):

1	2	3	4	
biggedy burn	**rig**gedy rubber	**when** I blabber	great.	I
miggedy make the	**Wond**er Twins	**de**acti-	vate.	It's . . .

There is a rest on the 4 beat of the first bar, followed by "great" punctuating the offbeat, both of which are highlighted. There is then a very slight pause before the word "I" begins and continues the lyrics, with "mig-" falling on the 1 beat of the second bar. So there is only a rest *before* the offbeat syllable, "great," giving it room to punctuate the offbeat.

This type of intricacy often comes out best when the rap is written to the specific beat that will be used for the track, rather than on a different beat, or without a beat at all.

Dray, Das EFX

For me, lyrics and beats are like if you go to the tailor and he custom makes a suit for you and it fits you perfectly, as opposed to you just went in and took a suit off the rack and it's a little baggy here, a little tight there. That's how my rhymes kinda feel when I lay them to a random track.

A Rest After the Offbeat Syllables

Alternatively, the offbeat syllables can be emphasized by putting a rest after them, but not before them. Again, this leaves enough space to break the continuation of the lyrics so that the offbeat can be punctuated effectively.

For example, here are two bars from Method Man's verse on Shaq's "No Hooks" (02:10):

1	2	3	4	
mindbender,	the death	**send**er to your	**ear**:	Method.
What up,	**hook**ers,	**hood** rats, and	**no**-gooders?	

"Ear" is said on the 4 beat, a short gap is left, then "method" punctuates the offbeat. It is then followed by a rest *after* it, creating enough room to allow it to punctuate the offbeat.

No Rests Surrounding the Offbeat Syllables

It is possible to punctuate the offbeat with no rests, though the effect isn't as obvious or prominent as when it is done using rests.

Here is an example from KRS-One's "MCs Act Like They Don't Know" (03:37):

1	2	3	4	
Cross your *T*s and	**dot** your *I*s when-	**ever**	I	ar-	**rive**.

Here, "I" punctuates the offbeat after the 3 beat. This is done by leaving slight gaps before and after the "I," breaking up the regular continuous flow of words, even though no actual rests are placed on the beats before or after it. This is combined with saying the "I" in a different way as well—the pitch is raised slightly and it's said with particular force.

Vast Aire, Cannibal Ox

It's not only what KRS-One was saying, but it was *how* he was saying it . . . it's not only what Chuck D was saying, but the dude had style. The subject matter could be the greatest thing ever, but if I don't want to hear it, then you're wasting your time. You could be saying, "Save the whales," you could be saying, "Recycle and don't litter," but if it wasn't done correctly, then you just wasted your time.

The same technique is used on the Pharcyde's "Ya Mama" (01:55):

1	2	3		4
Excuse me,	lady,	but	I re-	member seeing . . .

This can also be done by simply stressing some of the offbeat syllables or altering the pitch to make them stand out from the other syllables. This method does not create a really distinct punctuation of the offbeat though—the effect is a lot more subtle.

An Aside, Exclamation, or Noise on the Offbeat

A popular technique when placing syllables on the offbeat is to make it an aside or unrelated word, sound, or exclamation that doesn't fit or sound like it belongs in the previous sentence that has been rapped. This combines the surprise of syllables punctuating the offbeat (which is usually unanticipated) with some form of unexpected content.

Sean Price on "Fake Neptune" (00:25) uses this technique, using his popular "P!" exclamation on the offbeat:

1	2	3	4	
spliff with this	**bitch** trying to	**fasten** her	**pants**.	**P!**
Off	**with** her blouse and	**off** with the	**Kangol**. Vic- . . .	

Here, "P!" is said clearly on the offbeat, followed by a rest on the 1 beat of the second bar. It isn't part of the sentence before it or after it—it is a surprise exclamation punctuating the offbeat that listeners don't expect.

Sean Price, Heltah Skeltah

I got my signature things that I do that you know is Sean P, like most of my rhymes end off with "P!" or "motherfucker!" So you'll definitely have "P!" at the end of a rhyme or "motherfucker," I guess [that's] my exclamation point— "motherfucker." I got a tendency to stop in the middle of my bar and just be like, "psssh," something like that, I got my own signature things. [And] the beat tells me which way to touch it, I listen to the beat, I just don't try to force no flow on it.

Fast Burst of Syllables on the Offbeat

A fast burst of syllables, for instance using a triplet or fast 32nds, can be used to punctuate the offbeat in an interesting way.

Here is an example from near the end of Dr. Dre's "Day the Niggaz Took Over" (04:24):

1	2	3	4	
Listen to the	shots from my	nigga Doggy	Dogg,	bid-da-bye.
Dr.	Dre, him	bust gun-	shots.	

In this example, "Dogg" falls on the 4 beat of the first bar, and then a fast triplet, "bid-da-bye," punctuates the offbeat. This kind of unexpected element to add interest to a verse is also done with rhyme schemes, as we will see in chapter 3, p. 181.

Repeating Phrases with Different Rhythms

A technique that is often used on rapped choruses, but that can also be used in verses, is repeating a phrase and altering its rhythm the next time it is said.

Here is the main lyric from the chorus of Organized Konfusion's "3-2-1" (01:37):

1	2	3	4	
				three
strikes, two	tokes, one	time for the	mind.	

In the choruses, it is repeated three times with this rhythm, and then with a different rhythm for the fourth time. For example, this is the rhythm it changes to on the second chorus:

1	2	3	4
			three
strikes and two	tokes and	**one** time	**for** the mind.

When the same phrase is repeated, it is a lot easier to hear the change in rhythm—you know you're hearing the same words, but you also know there is something different about it. It draws your attention to the rhythm and the variation in the rhythm.

The technique is used in a similar way on the chorus to Quannum's track "Concentration," as well as on the Pharcyde's "Ya Mama" (02:23), in which one line is repeated in a different rhythm during one of the choruses, as shown here:

1	2	3	4	
				Ya
mama's gotta	**peg** leg	**with** a kick-	**stand.**	Ya
mama's gotta	**peg** leg		with a	**kick**stand.

As we can see, the line is repeated with a rest placed on the 3 beat, which shifts the words over so that "kick-" lands on the 4 beat, rather than "-stand," which did previously.

Altering rhythms in this way means that you have to be sure of how the initial rhythm goes and how the alternate rhythm goes—by either memorizing the rhythms, writing them down in a diagram, or recording them before they are forgotten.

Twista

Yeah, [I forget flows] all the time. A lot of times I will write a song too intricate or with a pattern and if I don't practice it over and over right then, I'll get to the end of the verse and then when I go back to the top of the verse to see how I said something, I [may have] forgot how I said it. I might have to change the line sometimes [because of that].

3/4 Time and Other Time Signatures

The vast majority of hip-hop beats are in 4/4 time, meaning there are four main beats in a bar, as shown in the flow diagrams with four beat numbers along the top. However, you can have beats with different numbers of beats in a bar—this is more common in other genres of music, such as jazz and classical music.

Here is an example of a rap in 3/4 time by Blackalicious, on the song "Chemical Calisthenics" (02:58):

1	2	3
Calcium	**plus** potass-	ium, mag-
nesium,	**news**paper	**of** sodi- . . .

This end part of the track uses a beat that has three beats in each bar, as shown by the three beat numbers along the top of the flow diagram instead of four. This means that each bar ends earlier than usual, so the MC has to adjust in order to place rhymes in the appropriate place (for example, if an MC would normally place a rhyme on the 4 beat, he or she would now have to place those rhymes on each 3 beat if each bar is to conclude with a rhyme).

With this way of rapping, the music or beat has to first be made with three beats in each bar, and then rapped to in that way. Similarly, a beat could be made with another number of beats per bar, such as five, and then an MC could rap in that time signature. The flow diagram would show five beat numbers along the top in that scenario.

This is another instance in which the beat will partially dictate how the flow will sound, because if the beat is in an unusual time signature, it will have to be written in a slightly different way than normal to get the flow to fit that timing. The MC would have to have the music first in order to do this.

Gift of Gab, Blackalicious

Usually I have the music first—for the Blackalicious stuff, Chief Xcel will give me a track, a skeleton of what the main beat of the track is gonna be, and then I'll write to that. Usually I'll go where the music takes me. I've really learned to just listen to the music and I kind of like to visualize where the music takes me, how the music makes me feel, what things the music makes me think about, and so I kinda just let the music guide me—I try to follow the music.

As very few hip-hop tracks use time signatures other than 4/4 time, this is an area that is wide open for experimentation and creative expansion.

K-Os

A good reason why my records sounded this way for the last two records, [*Joyful Rebellion* and *Atlantis: Hymns for Disco*, with] more different types of music, is just I'm having a very hard time getting excited by 4/4 time, just hip-hop. I've made so many that it wasn't exciting—it's only now that I'm starting to keep my ears open for different things. I think [different genres] coming into hip-hop is an exciting thing that might excite me a bit more to get into it that way.

2

Advanced Vocal Techniques

If you don't have a good voice and you don't know how to hit the beat right, then do something else, don't give us audio. The audio is very important. I want to be stimulated in my ears—that's why I do this.

◄ Evidence, Dilated Peoples ►

Although rhythm is perhaps the most indispensable aspect of MCing, as seen in chapter 1, the actual sound of an MC's voice—the vocal tone and use of vocal delivery techniques—is very important as well.

This is because the voice is the first element of MCing that listeners hear and judge you on—it is your first impression. Listeners immediately decide whether they like your voice or not and whether to keep listening. So in order to keep people listening, as Aesop Rock says, "You gotta have a voice that's unique and attractive."

Guerilla Black

Your performance is everything—your presence, your delivery of your actual verse is everything.

Andy Cat, Ugly Duckling

The history of hip-hop is filled with rappers who have distinct voices. In fact, it may be the most important element for a rap vocalist, [as suggested on] Gang Starr's song "Mostly Tha Voice," because that's the first thing a listener will hear and identify with.

As with rhythm, the vocal delivery is one of the elements of MCing that is often not given much thought or time. If you spend hours crafting complex rhyme schemes and incisive content, but then you don't put any time or thought into your voice and delivery, then many listeners will tune out before they even get to hear your content or rhymes.

Brother Ali

So much of it is the voice and feeling of hearing it. [That] adds so much to it, that I don't like reducing what I'm saying to writing. I put the lyrics in the little booklet for [one of my albums, but] even just looking at them I'm like, if you've never heard these, if you're only reading them, then I think you're missing a lot of it. It's not just solely the words.

Again, this is a reason some MCs record themselves coming up with improvised vocals as a way to begin writing a song, as we looked at with rhythm—if this is one of the elements that people will hear first, it can be a good idea to get it right first, before moving onto other elements. Recording the vocal as a way of beginning the writing process is also mentioned in the first *How to Rap*, pp. 147–149.

Gift of Gab, Blackalicious

I usually now keep a little recorder around, so when I write something, I'll spit it on the recorder just so that I can remember how I did it.

Vast Aire, Cannibal Ox
I like recorders, I mess with little recorders sometimes.

The quality of the voice is where a lot of the personality and individuality comes from. You can be a technically perfect MC in other areas, but if you are using a generic voice that doesn't stand out, with none of your unique personality coming through in the voice, then you can still sound bland even if you're rapping technically impressive rhythms, rhymes, and content.

E-40
I think [having a great] style has a lot to do with being an innovator—being unique and being different and separating yourself from the rest of the world and the rest of the rappers [in] the profession.

Speech, Arrested Development
Try to come original, come with something that's truly original and that truly feels like it's your own, that you can own. Those are the MCs that really impress me.

Depending on the type of voice you have to begin with, you may have to work harder on developing it and getting it to sound the way you want it to on your records than another MC who starts out with a great voice.

Shock G, Digital Underground
Know your own voice—be aware of what it can do and what it can't do. If you know your voice sucks or is mediocre, then you're gonna have to work harder than the next man. Prince has always had a "small," average voice, as opposed to husky and thick like James Brown, George Clinton, or Rick Ross, but look at all the sound he gets out of it! He's aware he has to put in work, and boy, does he. That was an R&B example, but the

very same thing applies to hip-hop. Know your voice—you might not be able to kick back and simply spell your name like Biggie did and still sound good.

Section A | Overall Voice Sound

Tone and Quality of Voice

The actual tone and quality of your voice is a very important factor in being an MC. As soon as you start rapping on a track, one of the very first things a listener will hear and judge you on, before you even get into any vocal techniques, is your tone of voice—which is, essentially, the overall sound of your voice. If you have a great, unique tone to your voice, listeners will be drawn to your music immediately, while if you have an unremarkable, forgettable voice, listeners may be put off immediately.

Guerilla Black
When you listen to 2Pac, his presence—dude could say nothing, he could say [nothing important in the content] for 16 bars, and you'd [still] be like, goddamn! Because of his presence, his delivery on the mic, his charisma came through—you knew that he was serious, absolutely serious.

David Banner
It's just like Pimp C from UGK, Pimp C may not be what people consider the biggest lyricist, but his style and his voice—I'd rather listen to him than somebody so called lyrical.

Innovation and uniqueness are huge parts of being considered a great, outstanding MC, and how your voice sounds is a large part of the equation. You can instantly recognize notable MCs from just a few words on a song—when 2Pac, Eminem, Kool G Rap, Slick Rick, Big Daddy Kane, Q-Tip, or Chuck D start rapping (and, of course, many other MCs, too), they can be recognized *instantly* on a song from their voice alone. If you don't sound distinct and memorable, or if you simply sound too much like someone else, it's very hard for listeners to pick you out of the crowd.

Big Daddy Kane

Basically just try being original, just be original. Throughout the years I've seen a lot of people that people have said, "Yo, he's nice," "Yo, he's ill," and it's like in my mind I'm like, "Yeah, but he sound just like this motherfucker."

Ordinary Voice Tone Versus Adapting Your Voice

Some MCs are able to use their regular voices in order to make an impact. For example, MCs such as Method Man and Slick Rick have voices that sound distinctive when they talk, so this translates well to their records without them having to alter their general tone too much.

Other MCs adapt their regular voices in order to stand out. For example, the Beastie Boys often rap a lot louder on records than they normally speak, and one of their members, Ad-Rock, often uses a higher pitch than his normal voice in order to create a very distinct vocal tone. B-Real of Cypress Hill also changes his voice to give it a more nasal tone when he's rapping, which is one of the most unique elements of the group's overall sound.

Del the Funky Homosapien

Whatever your voice sounds like, don't let nobody try to tell you "You don't have no rap voice" or some crazy stuff like that. It's how you use it. It's something that you can develop.

Andy Cat, Ugly Duckling

Some people "put on" a voice and it can be effective. I suppose the bottom line is this: if the rapper likes it and the audience likes it, why not?

It can take time to develop this adapted vocal tone, to create something that really works and fits in with the style of the beats and music that you're using.

B-Real, Cypress Hill

We had maybe five or six years of practice before we started actually recording to make a record. It took a while, it took us a few years before we even liked what we were doing, we were just trying things out. So finally when we got the sound that we liked, that's when we started to really go seriously hard on it.

Many MCs look to vocalists outside of hip-hop as well, to draw inspiration from and to model parts of their vocal delivery around.

Brother J, X Clan

I'm from the generation of those who dug in the crates—so much music has influenced me, performance-wise. You can think about music like Isaac Hayes—excellent production. I can go to my mother's old college crates and look at Barbra Streisand and get a lesson about projection. There's so many different areas of music when you're just listening to love music, so my influences go heavy, man. Funk is a very heavy influence on me, I love the freedom of funk music, you look at George Clinton, you look at Sly Stone, you look at Sun-Ra, you look at the monsters of the science of funk, man, that's a whole different beast, too. So I'm influenced by the ancestors and their creativity. I'm a universal listener of music, so you can hear classical music when I'm in my car, or see me with a Walkman on with some heavy metal, or I may be listening to some old school music or some new school instrumentals or whatever, however they divide it into these slots.

There are several elements that make up the tone of your voice, which we will look at. These include general pitch, volume, timbre, and other vocal characteristics.

General Pitch

Although the pitch of the voice can constantly change throughout a song, MCs usually have a general pitch that they stay around. This sometimes changes for MCs throughout their careers—Eminem had a relatively higher pitch on his earlier album, *The Slim Shady LP*, and then a lower general pitch on some tracks on later albums, such as on "The Way I Am."

Andy Cat, Ugly Duckling

You start learning what works for you and your voice. Say for my voice, I felt really drawn to stuff like the D.O.C., and Afrika from the Jungle Brothers, or Ecstasy from Whodini, because I like the really strong, rhythmic, soulful voice, and I felt like I could fit in that category, and that flow. I do most of the choruses and the hooks, kinda doing that same spirit, because I like a real solid voice.

It helps to study different MCs to see what sort of general pitches are used and which you enjoy, and then decide on the best general pitch to help make your voice sound original and distinct.

T3, Slum Village

Right now I think MCs should do the history, go back. Learn about some of these original rappers. The only reason why I say that is not saying it to be like school, but people need to respect rap a little more, all the new MCs coming up. Go back, listen to a couple of joints—there's some real guys out there. I think that once you listen to some of the old school and listen to a bit of the new school, [you can] then evaluate what you can add to the game.

Higher Pitch

Examples of MCs who use a relatively higher pitch than other MCs include B-Real of Cypress Hill, Eazy-E, Q-Tip of A Tribe Called

Quest, Bootie Brown of the Pharcyde, and Queen Latifah. A higher pitch often cuts through the other musical elements of the track well and is often used for playful, fun deliveries.

Andy Cat, Ugly Duckling

[Ugly Duckling group member Dizzy Dustin], he's got a little more high pitched and little more flavorful [vocal delivery], and a little more wily as far as his flow and doesn't do things as straightforwardly as I do. So you have to find out what [does and what] doesn't work for your voice type.

Mid-Pitch

Some MCs use a vocal pitch that isn't particularly high or low—Snoop Dogg, Tech N9ne, and Del the Funky Homosapien all have voices that aren't noticeably higher or lower than most other MCs' voices. This in-between type of pitch is usually done when an MC is simply using his or her regular voice on a track and it isn't really that high or low.

Lower Pitch

MCs who use a lower pitch than others include Rock from Heltah Skeltah, Wu-Tang Clan's Method Man, 2Pac, Chuck D of Public Enemy, Big Daddy Kane, CPO/Boss Hogg, and Scarface. A lower pitch often gives the voice more weight and authority, making it particularly effective when rapping about serious subjects.

Bootie Brown, The Pharcyde

I wanted to be like [Big Daddy Kane, but] unfortunately my voice wasn't as deep, [so] I wanted to be Big Daddy Kane mixed with Milk [from Audio Two]. Like, OK, I got a Milk-type voice, but I'll rhyme with Big Daddy Kane's flow—all that was me incorporating other people's styles.

Variations in Pitch

On top of this general pitch is the extent to which MCs will play around with the pitch—how much they will diverge from the default pitch of their voice.

Monotone Pitch

Some MCs don't change the pitch of their voice very much throughout a track—this is often called a monotone delivery, because just a single tone or pitch is used throughout most of the song. Although this is sometimes thought of as a negative thing (because it usually means there is less expression and variety, and so it can sound dull), it can work very well for certain MCs, as it can come across as a calm, steady, conversational tone. It can make the MC sound more laid-back, it can be used to show off a great beat (as it blends in and doesn't overpower it), and if the MC has a great voice in general, the listener may like listening to the voice at just one main pitch without too much variation.

A monotone pitch can make the verse sound more like percussion, as drum sounds tend to repeat a lot of the same pitches. It can also help to avoid making the delivery come across as too comical, which may happen with a lot of pitch variation.

Esoteric

I do feel keeping the same pitch helps the listener interpret the verse as rapid fire and hardcore. It certainly helps with keeping the flow and rhythm. In my opinion only a select few artists can really go high and low with their voices during an intricate verse and not sound corny.

MCs such as Nas and the late Guru of Gang Starr are great examples of a monotone delivery working really well—this is where the voice is memorable and enjoyable enough that the MC doesn't need to change pitch very often.

Del the Funky Homosapien

It depends on the song—the song might call for [a more monotone pitch]. I've heard some people say Guru was [too monotone], but he plays a purpose—you put him over that right beat, make that right song, he's perfect, can't nobody else do it but him. So it really depends what the atmosphere is and what that MC decides to do with his voice.

Other good examples of songs that work well with a steady vocal pitch include Divine Styler's "Ain't Saying Nothin'," Main Source's "Looking at the Front Door," and Eric B. & Rakim's "In the Ghetto." A monotone pitch can also be used for certain characters, such as those with robotic or alien voices—Devin the Dude's "Zeldar" (00:30) is an example of this.

Devin the Dude

[With the song] "Zeldar," it was a freestyle. When I started doing my verse it came out [sounding like an alien with a monotone delivery]—the beat was on and I just started free-styling like an alien. And when it was done, everybody was in there laughing and they were like, come [out of the vocal booth], and I was like, "Nah, I got to lay the hook, we ain't done yet!" [But the people in the studio said], "Nah, it's done, man, it's finished, that's it!" And I was like, "No, that's not it, I was just bullshitting!" Everyone was laughing and [enjoying the song as it was], so I was like, well, I'll just charge it to the game [and keep the "alien" freestyle as the finished track].

Changing the Pitch a Lot

Changing the pitch of your voice a lot is a great way to add personality, expression, and emotion to your delivery. This can be anything from making a few slight variations in the pitch just a handful of times in a song, to filling verses with loads of pitch variation, as MCs such as E-40 and members of the Pharcyde do, to give their vocals a lot of character. We will look at individual pitch techniques later on in this section (p. 95).

Zumbi, Zion I

I'm not the [type of MC] who writes hard battle raps [at one pitch] that can fit over anything—I probably could do that, but it's not really my style. I try to be as musical as I can, make it fit.

Sometimes changes in pitch occur through "mistakes" and accidental pitch changes due to natural fluctuations in your voice—however, these can sometimes be good and add to the overall individuality and character of the vocal.

Akir

I like little mistakes to be in my music here and there, just for a level of authenticity.

O.C., Diggin' in the Crates

Sometimes mistakes are good, sometimes you're looking for mistakes—it's just like it does something to the records.

Volume

The *volume* of your voice is how loudly or softly you're rapping—how much force you're putting into the vocals. This can be altered to some extent after recording a vocal take, because with studio equipment or programs you can change how loud the vocal is compared to the rest of the music. But the volume of your voice when you're actually delivering the vocals will still make a big difference to how they sound, no matter how they are mixed later on. This is because when you say something more loudly or softly, it creates different effects with your voice that can't be replicated by just mixing it in at a different volume.

Esoteric

This definitely makes a difference, because the louder you project your voice, the more it changes in sound and delivery. The volume can always be raised after the recording, but the pitch and style are shaped by the way you initially deliver the rhyme.

Tash, Tha Alkaholiks

When the microphone is on, it's like having a bullhorn in your hand. A bullhorn is one of them big horns that amplifies your voice if there's a rowdy crowd or something like that—you can push the button and everybody [can hear you]. The microphone is power, because you've got the microphone and you tell everybody, "Shut up," they're gonna look over and say, "Who said that?" You have power in your hands.

Different volume levels can also be used on a single track, altering the volume to suit the needs of particular rhythms or changes in content.

Shock G, Digital Underground

[I use] all three [volume levels] at times: lower, louder, and speaking volume. Depends, of course, on the sound we're going for.

Loud, Strong, and Forceful

Some MCs pick a louder, more forceful volume to rap at. This isn't as common a delivery as volumes that are closer to regular speaking level, but the MCs who do rap loudly are often very distinct because of it—KRS-One, Chuck D, Mystikal, and Melle Mel, among others, are all noted for their strong, powerful, and loud rapping voices.

Cutting Through the Musical Backing

A loud, strong, and forceful volume of vocals can work really well on tracks that are loud themselves and full of sounds—this is because a loud voice is needed to cut through all the things going on in the music. Chuck D is a great example of this—his vocals on Public Enemy's classic albums are able to force their way through the wall of sound. The Beastie Boys are also able to do this with their chanting style of delivery on very heavy beats such as "So What'cha Want."

Andy Cat, Ugly Duckling

Interestingly enough, I read a thing about Chuck D where he said he got a lot of his style because he liked sports a lot, and kinda like sports announcers, going, "YES!" Like Marv Albert as a basketball announcer in New York. So I think I like being drawn to that sort of excitement and the big announcement and the oratory power of it.

Being a Live MC

Moving the crowd and affecting a live audience (as described in the first *How to Rap*, pp. 289–310), is often easier if the MC has a loud, strong delivery. KRS-One, noted for being the epitome of a live MC, has very strong, clear, projected vocals, which come across effectively live, and the crowd hears and responds to everything he says.

Fredro Starr, Onyx

Doug E. Fresh got it, KRS-One got it, A Tribe Called Quest got it, Busta Rhymes got it, Onyx got it, DMX got it, there's a couple of [guys] who can rock shows, man, that I've seen.

Del the Funky Homosapien

It's more important than having good records—performances [are] the main way to "glorify your paper route," as my dude E-40 would say. If you can't come off as good or hopefully *better* live, you won't make it for too long. It seems like you fake or something if you sound good on record with Autotune and all of that, but on stage you sing horrible. You know? It just seems like it's only for the record and the money when it's like that.

Being a Party MC

Artists such as Lil Jon and Fatman Scoop are examples of a loud delivery being used to get a party atmosphere, especially where there is a call-and-response element (in which the MC chants one part of a lyric and the audience is meant to chant along or answer the chant). A softer-spoken MC will not usually have the same effect, as he or she might not be able to hype up the crowd and energize them in the same way a louder MC can.

Tech N9ne

Being able to know that it's about entertainment, being able to know that you've been to a KRS-One show and you seen people hopping to "The Bridge Is Over," you've been to a Public Enemy concert and seen people pumping their fists and hopping around. It's about having entertainment within your rap.

Giving Your Voice Authority

A louder voice often gives the MC a more authoritative sound, which is especially useful if you're trying to get a message or political point across or trying to teach the listener something. The louder and more confident an MC sounds, the more he resembles a teacher or someone making an important speech. This advantage of a louder vocal is seen on tracks by Melle Mel such as "The Message," as well as those by Chuck D of Public Enemy and KRS-One.

Andy Cat, Ugly Duckling

In the mid-'80s, Run DMC, Beastie Boys, LL Cool J, Kool Moe Dee—it was about being a powerhouse rapper and coming out with authority.

Yukmouth

A lot of times, [it's] like I didn't spit the verse powerful enough or strong enough and I gotta do it again, lay it more strongly, like when I was kinda light in the booth. There will be times like that when you're just lazy and do a lazy verse and need to re-lay it more stronger—there'll be times like that.

Short Phrases or One-Word Shouts

Sometimes a loud volume is useful for just one part of a verse, such as a loud shout or on a particular phrase. This is done on Queen Latifah's "Inside Out" (03:48) (she shouts, "Come now!"), Snoop Dogg's "Vato" (04:24), and Dr. Dre's "Day the Niggaz Took Over" (04:32) (he shouts, "Come again!" on both tracks), and by Mystikal on several of his tracks, such as on "Danger (Been So Long)" (00:11) (in which he shouts "Danger!" among other words and phrases).

One Be Lo, Binary Star

It's the difference between saying, "yeah," and "YEAH!" To me, that's a big difference.

Shock G, Digital Underground

If I'm doing a shout vocal, I imagine an audience in front of me or I imagine that I'm yelling down the street at someone blocks away.

Slightly Above Normal Voice Volume

A lot of MCs record vocals that are not extremely loud and force-ful, but are basically a slightly louder and more projected version of their regular voice. This means they don't come across as really loud, but it still gives their voice a sense of energy so that they don't sound like they're just speaking normally.

Del the Funky Homosapien

In real life I'm pretty much more laid-back than I am on the records. It's kind of different—I project it more when I rap.

Good examples of this include O.C.'s "Time's Up," in which he uses an amped-up version of his regular voice, while not going so far as to be really shouting out the lyrics, and Kool G Rap on "Men at Work," in which there is a vitality and presence to his voice due to the volume, again without him trying to be as loud as possible. It is important to be aware of volume in a live performance setting as well. Not every song has to be performed at the loudest volume possible.

Tajai, Souls of Mischief

Energy and appropriate energy for the track—I don't want to go to a performance where the guy is yelling at me the whole time, because every song is not like that on his album.

Still Sound Conversational, but with Energy

By keeping the volume closer to normal voice level, an MC can come across as more "conversational" to the listener—so that he or she seems more like a friend or colleague, rather than a teacher or public speaker. And when the volume is raised just slightly above normal, the vocal still retains a certain amount of energy and excitement that might be lost if it were kept at the normal speaking volume. The beat the MC is using may bring out this level of energy and volume.

Esoteric

When I recorded "Precision," I was very upbeat and animated, because the beat sounded like an all-out emergency.

Twista

[I'll go back and rerecord if the vocal doesn't quite have enough energy]. A lot of times I'll listen and I'll be like, you know what, I'm just not delivering that hard enough.

Good for Long, Impressive Verses

This level of volume and projection is good for longer verses that are meant to be a showcase of lyrics and techniques, because it's like an enthusiastic conversation rather than a lecture or an ordinary conversation. Examples of this are Rakim's "Lyrics of Fury," Big Daddy Kane's "Set It Off," and Kool G Rap's "Ill Street Blues." A lot of the classic, most well-respected verses and songs were done at this volume level, and it often requires great breath control (*How to Rap*, p. 239) to sustain the volume at this level.

Vursatyl, Lifesavas

It took years of me listening to all of the MCs that were great and I would commit their verses to memory and study how they did it, study what made them dope and tried to apply that to myself. It all came studying the great MCs, like Rakim and Slick Rick, Big Daddy Kane, Kool G Rap, Melle Mel, and KRS-One . . . [their best verses].

Royce Da 5'9"

I've always got the rhymes with a lot of words in them, where the flow is constant, so I gotta figure out where I'm gonna

take my breaths out in order to get it out and not compro-
mise certain lines with the delivery. I want everything to
sound strong, every word, every line. Sometimes it takes me
a long time, sometimes I'm in there until I'm getting fucking
hot and sweating, but I want my vocals to sound right.

Quieter and More Relaxed

Some MCs like to use a volume that is at their regular voice volume or even below—MCs such as Snoop Dogg, Q-Tip of A Tribe
Called Quest, and Slick Rick often rap at this volume level.

Del the Funky Homosapien

Q-Tip, the way he approaches it is more like a subtle or a
more sly way. So he's not as forceful as some other rappers,
but he still has a way of letting you know "Look, dude, I got
you!" It's just a subtler approach, a smoother tone. So I'm not
gonna say that you always gotta be forceful, because [there
are great MCs who aren't always forceful, such as] Q-Tip—he
doesn't really force it on you like that, he just approaches it
differently.

Relaxed and Calming

Some songs work best because they are relaxed and mellow, so
a lower vocal volume can work well on a laid-back track. A Tribe
Called Quest's "Bonita Applebum" uses this kind of volume, giving
the track a very casual and relaxed quality. The environment that
the MC is in while recording the vocal can also have an effect on
the volume, as can the beat.

Esoteric

[Sometimes it] depends on the mood of the beat I'm rapping on. Our song "Feel the Velvet" probably had my rapping
lower than I normally speak, because I was recording it in

my house at around 7 AM and the beat was really low-key and bass heavy.

Personality

Rapping at a regular speaking volume can sometimes allow MCs to be more "themselves" and have a wider range of emotion on a track. For example, if an MC raps mostly at a loud volume, it can be harder to get even louder for a part of a song that would work well if the volume was raised for just that part. Starting at a lower volume allows more room to get louder if needed.

Whispering

Whispering is normally used to add variety to the delivery or just for a specific section of a song, rather than as a common feature of an MC's overall style.

Adding Variety to the Delivery

Examples of whispering used on tracks are on Latyrx's "Storm Warning" (00:14 and 01:03), in which whispering is used on the chorus and the second verse, as well on the Pharcyde's "Ya Mama" (01:03) during one of the choruses ("Ya mama got a glass eye with a fish in it"). These sections break up the song and give the listener a change from the regular voices of the MCs.

Shock G, Digital Underground

[We have] lots of whispery tracks on "Sex Packets" and lots of whispery tracks on "Kiss You Back" too.

Sounding Atmospheric or Eerie

Whispering the vocals can make them seem eerier and more atmospheric. For example, at the end of Dogg Pound's "Dogg

Pound 4 Life" (04:16) there is a section of whispered vocals to give it an oddly evil-sounding vibe that fits with the rest of the track. Funkdoobiest's "Kc Sera Sera" (02:25) uses whispering during the chorus near the end of the track, making it sound more atmospheric for that section. Sometimes, this sort of whispered vocal is layered over a regular vocal take to give it this quality.

Planet Asia

Sometimes you want to punch in [or use other studio techniques, depending on] what kind of illusion you're trying to give off. That's what the studio is made for, for magic, to work magic and show illusions. [Like] when you're using a double-track and using other tracks to overlap—overlap a track, overlap a lyric.

Ying Yang Twins' song "Wait (The Whisper Song)" features vocals that are mostly whispered, and this is used as an overall concept for the delivery. Again, it gives the song an overall atmospheric quality.

Timbre

The timbre of the vocals refers to other qualities—besides pitch and volume—that make two voices sound different from each other. There are a number of different types of timbre, and it helps to be familiar with a lot of different MCs and their voices to be able to pick out the elements you like.

Zumbi, Zion I

I think the more people that you're exposed to, the more you can soak up in terms of what it's about, because you're not gonna have the complete package from the jump, you've gotta develop it.

To develop the timbre of your voice, it can help to practice with lyrics you have memorized, so that you can play around with the timbre without having to worry about what the words are.

Lateef, Latyrx

I do like to at least have one shot at a song with it memorized, because I feel like the way that I can play with the verse, in terms of what I can do with it tonally, increases and changes and has more range.

The timbre of the voice may further emphasize the personality of the MC (for example, a smooth voice may indicate a "smooth" persona), or it may be used as a contrast to the MC's personality.

Shock G, Digital Underground

People like George Clinton, Barry White, Professor X (R.I.P.) from X Clan, or Luther Vandross, [they're] smooth, romantic, and peaceful cats, but they have thick, gruff, and raspy voices. On the other hand, Eazy-E (R.I.P.), Eminem, and Huey P. Newton all boasted thin little voices, but also huge, explosive personalities and stage personas. It's common that a voice can be opposite [of] the personality, speaking strictly from a physical texture standpoint.

Although most MCs have a set timbre they use on most songs, some do alternate the timbre throughout certain tracks.

Andy Cat, Ugly Duckling

I also like to switch tones in the middle of a verse, especially when there's a musical change which might be a little more mellow than the music in the rest of the verse, [which is] an Ugly Duckling trademark. In [the track] "Turn It Up" [00:56], the middle two bars are very jazzy and cool compared to the main, rapping loop, so when I say, "When you rock this, let the fiber optics pound," I let my voice ease up a little to groove with the music. Then, when the main bit comes back in, Dizzy [Dustin] and I rap in more of an attack mode.

Nasal

Nasal sounds are any sounds that are partially produced through the nose. The most prominent example of this is B-Real of Cypress Hill's delivery, especially on Cypress Hill's earlier albums. To a lesser extent, a slight nasal tone is used by Eazy-E, Knoc-Turn'al (particularly on the chorus on Dr. Dre's "Bad Intentions" [01:02]), Ad-Rock of the Beastie Boys, and Rammellzee on parts of his song "Beat Bop" (05:20).

Croaky, Strained, and Unpredictable

Some MCs have a voice that is unpredictable and "croaky"—sounds break and fluctuate a lot. This is a large element of Lil Wayne's vocal style and to a lesser degree with RBX, and with the D.O.C. on tracks from his *Helter Skelter* album (made after an accident that damaged his vocal chords, altering his voice). MCs may also adopt this type of timbre if they feel it will suit a particular song.

Andy Cat, Ugly Duckling

We did a song called "Goodnight Now," where I waited until my voice was almost hoarse so I could capture a tired and sleepy sound to fit the theme of the tune.

A croaky delivery is sometimes created when rapping lower pitches that are not within an MC's normal range, as seen later in Pitch Techniques, p. 101.

Gruff

A gruffness—a kind of growly nature to the voice—is a natural element of some MCs' voices, which they often emphasize and accentuate on records. It often gives a warm character to the voice and suggests a level of maturity.

Wu-Tang Clan's Method Man has a lot of natural gruffness to his voice, making it instantly recognizable, as does DMX, Lyrics Born of Latyrx, and RBX. An example of a gruff delivery used to make a certain section of a song more distinct is on Cypress Hill's "Cock the Hammer" (01:35) during the parts after the main chorus.

Speech, Arrested Development

There's some artists to me [where] it's really not the lyrics that they're saying, it's more so their [voice or] swagger or their vibe that appeals to me in the first place. An example of that is Wu-Tang's Method Man, and I just like his vibe, it's the vibe of how he rhymes that I like.

Again, practicing a verse over and over so that you can focus on the delivery rather than trying to remember the lyrics is a good way of then going on to develop the timbre.

RBX

To me, my character and the strength of my voice and the whole thing that I bring to the table is strengthened when I know it, and when I'm confident with it, and I can actually jump into the creases and crevices of the track—that's always better.

Smooth

If a vocal isn't gruff, croaky, or raspy at all, the sound usually comes out very smoothly. This often produces a nice, warm, uninterrupted, level sound, which is particularly good for songs with a relaxing quality (such as songs by Q-Tip and Snoop Dogg) and songs with a "ladies' man" theme (such as songs by Big Daddy Kane). A "smooth"-sounding beat may also inspire a smoother approach to the vocals.

Esoteric

If the beat is made of soft drums and a smoothed out jazzy vibraphone, you might want to take a more laid-back approach.

Tash, Tha Alkaholiks

If I hear a beat that sounds like I should rap [in a particular way] on the beat, that's what I go with. If it's a rowdy beat we rap rowdy, if it's a smooth and mellow beat we might [match the beat with smoother vocals].

Planet Asia

It's gotta sound smooth, man, I'm all about sounding fresh.

A smooth timbre may also help an MC blend well with other instruments in the track.

Crooked I

Every beat, every instrumental, has a way that you can rhyme over the top of it better. When I listen to it, I [might] say, "OK, this beat right here, there's a lot of instruments in this beat." Therefore, since I don't have a husky, Busta Rhymes voice, I'm gonna have to approach this instrumental in a way to where I'm using my voice so I would sound like one of the instruments, instead of me cutting against it. [I'm] actually flowing with the beat.

Harsh, Sharp, Raspy

Some MCs use a harsher, raspier sound when they rap, almost as if they're close to losing their voice due to the coarseness of the sound. Mystikal uses this kind of delivery, and it makes him very easy to immediately recognize on a track—this gives the vocal a lot of energy and a kind of manic charisma and personality in most cases. It may be hard to "put on" more rasp if your voice isn't naturally raspy.

Shock G, Digital Underground

I've always wished I had more rasp, but I know there's no point in wasting thought on that. It is what it is.

Breathy

A breathy timbre can be achieved by adding a lot of breath and extra air as you say the vocals. An example of this is the delivery of the late MCA of the Beastie Boys—the breathy quality gives the vocals a lot of character and a relaxed, laid-back vibe.

Esoteric

The subject matter affects the voice, too. If you are rapping about a girl, you are going to be a little more humane, and if you are rapping about taking a man's head off, you gotta sound like you mean it.

Other Vocal Characteristics

Additionally, some MCs have unusual vocal characteristics that make them instantly recognizable.

Aspects that are sometimes considered speech impediments can actually be advantages in MCing. Things like lisps and mis-pronunciations can add a lot of character and individuality to a vocal delivery.

For example, Kool G Rap's lisp is an integral part of his overall vocal style, even though it's simply an inherent part of his voice. It also makes his clear, precise, and often fast use of many compound rhymes even more impressive, as they are said with a vocal condition that may otherwise obscure words. RBX also has a slight lisp, as well as an unpredictable vocal tone, and this adds a huge amount of individuality and character to his voice.

RBX

In a world where everybody is pastel, it's always [good] to have some real [strong] color.

After 50 Cent's shooting incident, his voice was altered so that his speech was slightly slurred. This may have made him more distinct and recognizable on record, and his commercial success came largely after the event. The D.O.C.'s vocal chords were damaged in a car accident, and this changed his voice completely, as can be heard from his first album, *No One Can Do It Better*, to his albums after the accident, such as *Helter Skelter*.

So rather than trying to smooth out or eliminate a vocal condition or oddity, it can sometimes be more effective to keep it in and make it an element of your vocal style that makes you stand out.

Fredro Starr, Onyx

Rule number one—don't bite. That's rule number one in rap, don't bite, you gotta have originality. You gotta bring something new to the game and stay original.

Lord Jamar, Brand Nubian

My advice would be to find your own voice and your own story, whatever it is, and be truthful, because hip-hop likes the truth. Back in the days, you couldn't sound like the next man, they'd say you were biting.

Occasionally, other factors may alter your voice from day to day, such as a sore throat or being tired. These things often add another element of interest if you decide to record vocals on the day they occur, and they can sometimes be used to your advantage.

Shock G, Digital Underground

Throat health, muscle fatigue, stress level, level of comfort with surroundings, intoxication, dehydration, emotional state, confidence, even the humidity and altitude at which you happen to be recording or performing can all affect the sound of your voice. Drastic differences due to any of the above can occur from one day to the next. If you compare recordings done on different days, even with the same mic and input settings, you can notice and compare the different "yous." So yes, I think my voice can help my personality get across, when the many variables are stacked in my favor. Some, even most, of those things can be controlled through vocal training and artistic professionalism, but certain ones, like confidence, emotional state, stress levels, comfort, can't be faked or controlled. [Sometimes I may have to tell myself,] "Just walk away and reschedule, Shock! It ain't going down today!"

Accents, Impressions, Characters

Accents

Accents are more important in rapping than they are in regular singing. Many singers put on a generic accent to sing with and to hold longer notes, so their "normal" accent often isn't focused on. With rapping, MCs often sound closer to how they normally speak, so an accent will be heard more clearly.

Listeners immediately get certain information from your accent, such as what country you're from and which region in that country. Some accents are so specific it can narrow the MC's background down to a very small area if someone is familiar with that particular accent. An accent may even be held against someone, if a listener decides he or she doesn't like hip-hop from a particular place and he or she hears that accent on a record.

David Banner

This is gonna be powerful and I hope it's not taken the wrong way, but I think people connect lyricism with the closer you are to sounding like you're from New York. Even if you look at the Southern rappers who are the most successful [criti-cally], it's the ones that sound more like they're from New York and who sound least like they're from the South. With me being from the South, I still gotta prove myself as a lyri-cist every time.

Esoteric

There are certainly very talented MCs that write and deliver amazingly well, [but] that I don't listen to due to their accents. It comes down to personal preference. Rakim and EPMD are pioneers that fit my description of what hip-hop is supposed to sound like, so my tastes are rooted in artists that sound like them.

Certain accents may give an MC more character than other accents. For example, Slick Rick's mix of an American and English accent is unusual, so it is one of the defining characteristics of his style. Some MCs have a strong country accent that adds a twang to everything they say and rap, while others may have a more generic accent that doesn't add or detract from the rest of their rapping style.

Some accents go hand in hand with a certain flow, like a Jamaican accent with a more rapid-fire, ragga-style flow that includes a lot of triplets (see p. 16 for more on triplets).

2Mex, The Visionaries

I like to hear people talk that are different from the usual scene . . . from Europe, from all over the world, so I can be like, "Oh, that's how they talk?" and their rhythms.

Using Your Normal Accent

Using the accent you normally have when you speak is often popular with MCs who like to keep their subject matter and overall identity as true to real life as possible. If your lyrics are all about where you grew up and your real life experiences, then it would probably be counterproductive to put on a different accent to rap with. Also, your "real" accent may be distinct enough already, so that you don't need to change it at all to stand out.

Esoteric

I have experimented in the past, but it doesn't work for me. I keep it as real as I can with my voice, so if I am delivering a laid-back verse, then that is probably as close to my speaking voice as it is going to get. In the late '90s, I had no idea [about my accent] until I started hanging with Vinnie Paz [of Jedi Mind Tricks] and the rest of Army of the Pharoahs. They made sure to point the Boston accent out and it made me much more conscious of it. I focused on it for a few months, to the point I was developing a complex about it, but then I forgot all about it again. It gives me something most other cats don't have. It isn't something I think about anymore when I record. I just rhyme and it comes out how it does.

Immortal Technique

Don't be afraid to be yourself. Everything about me is me. I don't play a character when I get on stage.

David Banner

I want to hear stuff that relates to my everyday life and somebody that speaks and has gone through the struggle and the struggle connects us.

Using a Different Accent

There are several reasons why you might want to adopt a different accent—it's not always a bad thing to stray away from your regular accent or voice.

Lateef, Latyrx

I think it's kind of limiting to go, "Oh, it's gotta be real," because a lot of ideas are good that aren't real. Anything that I come into contact with [can influence the style]. Fictional stuff can easily be part of what I'm talking about—I could watch a sci-fi movie and write a song about it.

You may want to create an alter ego and give the "character" you have created a different style. Or while developing a unique delivery for yourself, you may want to put on a different accent to stand out from the crowd.

El Da Sensei

Don't be scared, really explore your mind and be different. Coming up, you never wanted to bite, you never wanted to copy nobody's style. Don't break the laws of being an MC, because once you do that, who are you now? You're not really an MC, you're just a copycat. So I try to tell cats be as original as possible.

Cage

The only way to be hip-hop in any of this sort of thing would be to be unlike [everyone else]. Be innovative, that's what I learned about rap music, hip-hop, [it's] very much like punk rock. It was very aggressive, it was very DIY, it was making shit cool—inventing [things].

You may want to do it for humorous reasons—Eminem sometimes adopts a fake vaguely French accent, as on "Under the Influence" (00:01), in which he also makes up some foreign-sounding noises to go with the accent, and the Beastie Boys do English accents on the track "Triple Trouble" (00:01) to give it a lot of humor.

It can be used for a specific character in a story rap, when you're portraying another character who has a different accent. There are also many examples of MCs who don't normally have Jamaican accents, but who adopt one to do a ragga-influenced section of a song, to add to the style.

Shock G, Digital Underground

I believe we all can do accents and voices, we just don't all try to, or don't allow ourselves to for fear of losing our respect. It's not a rare or special talent it requires, but a type of personality that doesn't care how it looks, or that doesn't believe their respect will be compromised in any crucial or lasting way.

Doing a Different Region's Accent

Within a country, you can have a number of different regional accents, such as New York, Midwestern, and Southern accents in the United States and Southern and Northern accents in England. Different accents say different things about an MC, as certain regional accents convey different information.

A Brooklyn accent might give a feeling of city life, while a Texan accent might evoke a more open, country feel on a song. Kool G Rap's accent helps him convey the pictures he's painting of street life on tracks like "Streets of New York" and "Ill Street Blues," while the Southern accents of Bubba Sparxxx and Nappy Roots give their tracks a country feel. On Snoop Dogg's "Tommy Boy" (00:09), he puts on a Southern accent at the beginning of the track, as he is paying homage to the South.

Esoteric

Domestically, your accent can help you . . . it depends on what region is hot at the time.

If you have an accent that is already from a popular area and you don't alter it, it may be harder to stand out, but as long as you're innovating in some other area of your MCing, it doesn't have to hold you back.

Pigeon John

Out of Queens you have Run DMC, Q-Tip, LL Cool J, and 50 Cent and Mobb Deep, and all these different types of characters from one city, out of L.A. you have N.W.A. and the Pharcyde from the same neck of the woods [and they still all managed to be different from each other and original].

Doing a Different Country's Accent

The same applies with countries—a French accent might suggest more culture and romance, while an Australian accent may suggest a fun, outdoors environment.

Examples of MCs putting on a British accent include the Beastie Boys on "Triple Trouble" (00:01), in which it's done mostly for comedic effect, Dana Dane putting on a semi-British accent as part of his overall style, and the beginning of Big Daddy Kane's "Show and Prove" (00:59), when a line is said in an English accent as part of a punch line ("I don't think so, mate"). Using a different country's accent also usually involves using some of their slang and phrasing as well.

Lateef, Latyrx

I've done songs with people from Britain, and I'm obviously American and there will be some word usage that I'll use that they don't really say. [They will be like,] "We don't really say that here."

A lot of MCs put on a Jamaican accent at times, especially when rapping in a more ragga/reggae type of style. Eminem does this accent on "We as Americans" (02:49) ("Automatic and no one gon' test this, mon, clack, click"), Lauryn Hill does it on "Lost Ones" (00:33), Slick Rick does it on "Love That's True Part 2" (00:14), and KRS-One does this accent on "Sound of Da Police" (02:42).

Sometimes having a foreign accent may count against an MC, though, or make it hard for the MC to be accepted by certain audiences.

Esoteric

Sometimes words will come out with a New York accent because several artists were raised on New York hip-hop, and that's the blueprint—I do highly respect it when MCs from other countries keep it authentic and do not try to imitate the New Yorkers, though. [Having a foreign accent can be] a huge disadvantage on an international scale, [and] lots of talented MCs suffer from this. It shouldn't be that way, but it is.

Making Up an Accent

An accent can be made up, often using a combination of random sounds from other accents. Eminem does this on the very beginning of "Under the Influence" (00:01)—he then offers a "translation" of his made-up accent and lyrics immediately afterward, in the song.

Impressions of Other People or Characters

Sometimes MCs do impressions of other MCs or other famous people or characters. This is almost always done for entertaining or humorous effect, as they usually aren't actually trying to convince listeners that they *are* that person; they're doing it because it'll sound interesting or funny.

Eminem has a number of tracks in which he does impressions of other people or characters. These include an impression of Snoop Dogg on the track "Bitch Please II" (02:32) (the lines beginning, "Oh no, big Slim Dogg . . ."); Triumph the Insult Comic Dog on the track "Ass Like That" (01:10) (throughout the song, for example in the lines "For I am Triumph, the puppet dog, I am a mere puppet, I can get away with anything I say, and you will love it"); and characters from the television show *South Park* on the track "The Kids" (00:01).

Del the Funky Homosapien

Everything helps. I grew up doing impressions and stuff, like "Heavens to Murgatroyd!" [*said in the voice of the cartoon character Snagglepuss*]—I grew up watching a lot of cartoons. It helps making it entertaining, like that voice, Snagglepuss, I just did it on a song I did [recently]. Gave it to my girl, she was, like, dying laughing. So anything you could throw into the pot adds more to your personality. I would say you better try to get every bit you can, every little bit and nook and cranny inside you, and try to throw that in the pot, because anything you throw in there is just going to make it more likely that you will succeed.

Other cartoon characters are impersonated by Funkdoobiest, imitating Sylvester the Cat's catchphrase, "Sufferin' succotash" on their track "Super Hoes" (02:38) and Fu-Schnickens performing an Elmer Fudd–styled line of "Come back here, bunny wabbit" on their track "Sum Dum Munkey" (01:31). Shock G's alter-ego voice (looked at further on p. 93) is based on a cartoon character.

Shock G, Digital Underground

"Hip Hop Doll" (00:11) was the first time I tested what later became the "Humpty" voice, and I was actually imitating the Warner Bros frog [Michigan J. Frog, singing "Hello My Baby"], who himself was imitating the oldies pop singer Bing Crosby.

Doing these types of impressions often requires a sense of humor and a willingness to let go and not care how you may be judged for it.

Shock G, Digital Underground

I think my predominant essence is like that of a comedian, because my natural at-rest mental state is more giggly-goofy-jokey than it is "need people to take me serious" [or] "[I] need to fit in" minded. But most rappers want to be taken seriously, and it's the pursuit of that serious respect that doesn't allow for any "silly" impressions or any visible break in their serious "true" self—that concern that it could make them appear weak to the fans and therefore jeopardize the mission!

Del the Funky Homosapien

Some people is, like, too good for that, they don't wanna do that, but I feel like if you let loose and you're just loose sometimes, it engages people more. It allows people to feel kinda comfortable, and like, "OK, it's not that serious." I try to keep the mood of it [like], "OK, I got something to say, but it ain't that fucking deep." It's not that serious—I'm just trying to have some fun with you for a minute and then you can go back to whatever you were doing. You don't [always] want somebody to listen to your [music] and they feel like it's a drag—like, man, this is like the doom of the world. And don't get me wrong, I've done songs, I'm sure, where the feel was like that, but naturally I just got a sense of humor, so that's the way I come about it. You gotta be loose and open and free enough, because if you're not, them ideas won't come out. You'll be too scared to do it.

Sometimes this is done in homage to another MC or person, such as on A Tribe Called Quest's "If the Papes Come" (00:24) when Q-Tip quotes and mimics the beginning of Slick Rick's

"Children's Story." This is also done at the beginning of Wyclef Jean's "Bubblegoose" (00:11) mimicking the same Slick Rick song ("Hey kids, gather around, I got a story to tell, here we go").

Akil the MC, Jurassic 5

If you have a knowledge of different types of MCs, then that helps you be able to pick your lane, or helps you create your own lane, as opposed to just driving recklessly over lanes that are already there.

Different Character Voices

Instead of impersonating real people or fictional characters from other sources, some MCs create their own characters for a song or series of songs. This can add a lot of vocal variation to a song, though some MCs caution that you can't lean on this too heavily as the only point of interest.

Shock G, Digital Underground

Different characters add to the variety, but variety alone doesn't guarantee something's interesting. There's a lot more variety in the dollar store, for instance, than, say, Guitar Center or the Apple store, but who's more interesting?

Story Rap Characters

Often, these can be the voices of various characters in a story rap. Slick Rick does this sort of change of voice for different characters in a lot of his story raps—for example, in his song "Children's Story" (00:11, 01:01, 01:08, and 01:49) he begins and ends the song with kids' voices ("Uncle Ricky, would you read us a bedtime story?") and during the main body of the song he does a police character's voice ("Keep still, boy, no need for static"), and the main character's voice ("Why'd you hit me?"; "I need bullets, hurry up, run!"). Often, these different character voices are *punched in,* a technique explained in *How to Rap,* p. 274.

Vast Aire, Cannibal Ox

I do one takes, I also do punch-ins—I find that different songs are different songs. I was just listening to Slick Rick last week, and his albums wouldn't be the same if he didn't punch. So different lines or different songs need a particular flavor.

Male/Female Voices

A good way to use a different voice to make the vocal more interesting is to use a voice of the opposite gender. So if you're a male MC, do a female voice for a line in a story or scenario, and if you're a female MC, do a male voice during a verse. Eminem does this on the track "The Real Slim Shady" (00:44), saying "Yeah, but he's so cute though" in a girl's voice, and Slick Rick does it several times on the song "Sittin' in My Car" (01:21), for example with the line, "Well if you ain't love her, why'd you go back to bed with her?"

Random Characters to Interact With

Doing a different voice is sometimes used to show that someone else is talking in a scenario. For example, Doug E. Fresh does this on "The Show" (03:40) by changing his voice in the part of the song when he answers the phone ("Hello, is Doug E. Fresh in?"/"No, he's not in right now"). He uses two different voices for the caller and the answerer of the phone—neither are a specific type of character in a story; they're simply different characters in the brief scenario in the song, and the voices are done to make it interesting and so you can tell there are two people rather than just one.

Notorious B.I.G. also raps as a different character on the phone on the song "Warning" (00:39), as does Wyclef Jean on "Bubblegoose" (01:04)—both tracks use a phone effect added onto the vocal later for the "other" character, to differentiate that character from the main character.

Stezo does the technique on the track "It's My Turn" (02:45) near the end of the track, when a different voice is used to ask himself a question ("Why Stezo?") and the other voice is simply used to show that it's meant to be another person asking the question.

It often helps to have a good audio engineer to make these back-and-forth vocals sound seamless.

Del the Funky Homosapien

With that song ["Time Is Too Expensive," going back and forth with my own voice], I did a lot of work. Matt Kelley, actually, the engineer, helped me do a lot of stuff on that song, so I gotta give some shout outs to Matt Kelley, who taught me a lot about recording, just watching him or asking questions—he's an excellent engineer. He made a lot of suggestions, he recorded all the vocals, he knew how to get what I was talking about, in the studio. And that's what an engineer needs to be able to do, so really it was the engineer's magic that made it happen, because I just had the idea, but I didn't quite know how to do it. Matt Kelley was the one that knew how to get the sound that was in my head onto tape and how to do it quickly. So it took a little bit of razzle-dazzle, the studio magic, to make it happen. You gotta kind of know your way around the studio to make it happen.

Doing Your Own Voice in an Earlier or Different Situation

Sometimes a slightly different voice is used to show when it's something the same MC has said previously or in a different situation. For example, on 2 Live Crew's "Me So Horny" (00:56), group member Brother Marquis raps, "Dialed the 7 digits, said, 'Yo, this Marquis, baby! Are you down with it?'" using a slightly altered voice to indicate that the "Yo, this Marquis . . ." part was something he said in an earlier situation.

Similarly, Boogie Down Productions' "Love's Gonna Get'cha" (04:48) includes the line, "I threw the gun down and began to shout, 'Come on, I got 'em!'" where the "Come on . . ." section is said in a louder voice, which makes it clear he's quoting himself in an earlier scenario. Again, this technique is often done with punch-ins, to record it more effectively.

Zumbi, Zion I

[I do it in] one take, unless I'm styling it with the punch-ins, like a Slick Rick style, or Redman does it sometimes, like coming back and answering myself on another track. That way I'll definitely punch.

Alter Egos

An alter ego is an alternate personality that someone creates for themselves. This can be a clever way to keep the listener interested, by essentially creating a whole new MC—for example, in Digital Underground, which already has group members Shock G and Money B, there is also a third MC: Humpty Hump. Humpty Hump is a character created by Shock G, using a different voice, and he has several of his own "solo" tracks, as well as "interacting" with Shock G on some tracks.

Shock G, Digital Underground

I was clear on what I wanted to hear, so I would just do the parts myself to keep from losing it in translation. Humpty [Hump] was a rapper I myself wanted to see and hear, but nobody else was doing it, so I just did it myself. Some experimenting happened before Humpty arrived on the Digital

Underground set. It was a gradual evolution; each next feature added a new piece to his eventual look and persona.

While developing an alter ego, there may be interplay between the creation of the character's personality and "look," as well as the character's "voice."

Shock G, Digital Underground

The voice came first, on [the song] "Hip Hop Doll" (00:11), but I only sang choruses with it. Then a few months later I penned "Doowutchyalike" (00:17) and took the voice a little further by allowing "him" to rhyme this time, since people were feeling the froggy, Bootsy Collins, Slick Rick–meets–Rodney Dangerfield voice. [It's] absolutely a different emotion [when I'm in character as Humpty]—it's called the "goopty!" state of mind. And I swear, half of it is in the outfit—put on a loudly colored plaid or polka-dot suit, a tall fur hat, and a nose and glasses disguise, and then watch how differently you rhyme and dance while you wear it!

This is especially useful if you're a solo artist, because it brings more elements to your songs. Eminem has his Slim Shady persona, with a more cartoony, animated vocal tone, as well as his regular voice. It can be done for just one song as well—Notorious B.I.G. creates an alter ego on "Gimme the Loot" (00:30), doing a higher pitched vocal for the alter ego character he's rapping and interacting with.

An alter ego may even be believed to actually be another, real MC for a time, if the voice is different enough from the MC's regular voice.

Shock G, Digital Underground

The alter ego thing was mostly just for fun. It emerged pretty easily and naturally, and I didn't really think about how it might make things better or worse down the road. We all felt it was working—the group, the audience, the label—so we rolled with it. There was this Peter Parker/Spider-Man fun secrecy about it that we all shared, even 2Pac and Money-B. They were [like] the superheroes with one consistent identity, while Shock and Humpty functioned more like Bruce Wayne and Batman. We all had fun protecting the illusion, and we all were entertained by the extent to which it was working.

Section B | Specific Techniques

Pitch Techniques

In addition to an MC's general pitch, which we looked at earlier as part of the overall tone of the voice, there are many individual techniques and uses of pitch. Some MCs plan out their use of pitch before they record their lyrics. It can be memorized in their heads, written down in some way, or recorded as they come up with the delivery. Other MCs improvise their use of pitch while they're doing the final recording.

Brother Ali

For me, when I know something is gonna work, I hear the music and I hear what my voice is sounding like on it. I don't necessarily hear the words, but I hear the delivery and the tone and the pitch. When I hear it [sounding good] in my head, I know it's [going to be] good [on the record].

Changing the Pitch on a Syllable or Word

A very common technique is to change the pitch on a particular word or syllable. This is one of the most popular vocal delivery techniques in order to give the vocals more character and expression. MCs who have a lot of expression and character in their voices, such as Snoop Dogg, Pharoahe Monch of Organized Konfusion, and E-40, use changes in pitch a lot more than other MCs, as it is a strong way to add character and personality to the delivery.

Del the Funky Homosapien

This is why artists can get away with saying nothing, basically, and still have a hot song—lyrical density or deep meaning as far as the public's perception comes *after* they like the song enough to even dig that deep. The first layer of musical pleasure is the sheer enjoyment of the sound of the music itself.

Higher Pitch on a Syllable or Word

Using a higher pitch on a certain word is used in different situations to create various effects. Even though it is sometimes a relatively subtle technique, it can make a big difference to the overall feel and entertainment value of a verse.

To Add Character and Variety

A higher pitch on a word is generally used to create variety throughout a verse. Otherwise the pitch would stay pretty much the same for the entire song, and this can be dull and uninteresting for the listener.

Snoop Dogg uses this on his song, "Who Am I (What's My Name)?" (01:25), in which he raps, "Niggas can't fuck with this and niggas can't fuck with that," raising the pitch in both instances of the word "fuck" to make the line very distinct and memorable. The second verse of South Central Cartel's "Sowhatusayin'" (00:58) has a high-pitched syllable near the start, in which the lyrics "the o-riginal from the block" are said with a high pitched "o" sound on the word "original," so that the verse begins in a very memorable way.

The music may be a source of inspiration for this kind of change in pitch—it may make the MC think of a certain type of delivery style.

Pusha-T, Clipse

Certain beats make me think of certain things, like [the beat for the track] "Momma I'm So Sorry" put me in the spirit of [the Notorious] B.I.G., so with that being said, it's like some of the fluctuations in my vocals and shit like that, it sort of came from there.

To Emphasize a Point

Sometimes a word is raised in pitch to emphasize a point or argument being made in the content of the verse. For example, Chuck D on Public Enemy's "Fight the Power" (01:46) raps, "No, we're not the same," raising the pitch on "no" as he's arguing his point to the listener and emphasizing the "no." This kind of technique can often be developed after memorizing the lyrics.

Chuck D, Public Enemy

It would be a great help if you do have it memorized, because you can play around with it more. Certain things that I do have memorized, I can come up with a lot of different inflections that I wouldn't necessarily come up with reading [the lyrics].

Likewise, on Snoop Dogg's "Murder Was the Case" (03:04) is the line "'Cause you can't tell what's next," where "you" is slightly raised in pitch to emphasize his point that "you can't tell what's next."

To Persuade Someone to Do Something

Pitch is sometimes raised in order to express a need for someone to do something—to persuade someone through emotion. This is done on A Tribe Called Quest's "Bonita Applebum" (00:27). In the chorus, he says "gotta put me on" at a steady, level pitch first. Then when he repeats the phrase, he raises the pitch on "gotta" ("you gotta put me on") as he is trying to persuade the girl in the song that she *has* to "put him on."

Del the Funky Homosapien

I was born in '72, right, [and] back then what rapping meant, basically, was you trying to convey something—you're trying to *convince* somebody. That's what rapping is, it's in the way you talk.

To Sound Scared or Confused

Pitch is often raised on a syllable when the MC wants to sound scared or confused as part of the delivery—for example, in the context of a story rap in which he or she is portraying a character who is scared or if the MC wants the listener to clearly hear the emotion in the delivery.

On Organized Konfusion's "Thirteen" (00:26), on the lyrics "Run when you hear it," the pitch is raised on the word "run," giving it a scared sound, suggesting that the listener should get the emotion of fear while hearing the line. On Snoop Dogg's "Murder Was the Case" (01:00), his line "Damn, I see demons" raises in pitch at the end, because his character in the story is seeing demons and is afraid.

Pharoahe Monch

I try and embody the scared-ness and the live-ness of being at a festival with 50,000 people every time I go in the studio. I put that pressure on myself to make these songs come out the way that they do, knowing that eventually I'm going to have to perform them, so that's what I take in mind when I'm in the studio.

When Asking a Question

When asking a question, we normally raise the pitch at the end of a sentence, to indicate that it is a question. This means that when a question is asked as part of a rap verse, it normally alters the delivery, because the pitch has to be raised to show that it is a question. This happens on Snoop Dogg's tracks "Murder Was the Case" (01:18) ("Will I be the G that I was?") and "Serial Killa" (02:15) ("Now tell me, what's my motherfucking name?")

Lower Pitch on a Syllable or Word

As well as raising the pitch on a particular syllable or word, the pitch can also be lowered. This has a similar effect of creating variation, as well as having some different effects to raising the pitch.

To Add Character and Variety

As with raising the pitch, one of the main uses of lowering the pitch on a syllable or word is to make the delivery more varied and interesting. For example on Organized Konfusion's "Stress" (02:32) the phrase "these wack MCs" is said with the pitch lowered for the "Cs" part of the word "MCs," just to make the delivery more entertaining and unpredictable for the listener.

Andy Cat, Ugly Duckling

I like to vary the pitch in my voice when it is useful in getting across a vibe or emotion. Many vocalists stay in the same range when they rap and those who do tend to use a more aggressive and percussive tone. But I think, as a vocalist, it's important to use every range you've got when presenting lyrical ideas; especially over the span of an album.

To Sound Serious and Give More Authority

Going down in pitch in regular speech is a way to make a statement, and this technique is often used when the speaker is more serious or wants to project more authority.

Snoop Dogg on "Tha Shiznit" (02:05) does this to end one of the verses, rapping "'Cause Snoop Dogg is the shit." The lowering of the pitch on the word "Dogg" gives the line more weight and seriousness than if the pitch stayed the same or was raised.

On Organized Konfusion's "Maintain" (00:23), the line "Sitting at the edge of my bed and I'm fed" ends with the pitch lowered on the word "fed," which sets the mood for the track, in which the MC is serious and talking about a serious subject.

To End a Line

Lowering the pitch on the last word of a line is often a good way to make the line sound "final," especially if it is the last line of the verse or song. This is done on the D.O.C.'s "Funky Enough" (00:43) at the end of the verses, where "funky enough" has a lowered pitch on the word "enough," to give it the feel that the verse is over and the chorus is about to begin.

Omar Cruz

An inflection [or change in pitch]—if I'm gonna say something in a certain way, I'll maybe darken it in a little bit [when I write it down]. These are the things that you pick up as a writer, everyone has [them], like when people were in school they had different note-taking styles.

Croakiness and Lower Pitch

Often when going down to a lower pitch, there is a certain "croaky" quality given to the sound, as it's hard to get a very smooth, deep sound unless you have a naturally deep voice or a vocal range that lets you go smoothly down to a lower pitch. However, this croakiness gives the sound an extra level of character and isn't something that needs to be "fixed" or smoothed out in most cases.

A very clear example of this is on Snoop Dogg's "Tha Shiznit" (02:44) in the line "Lay back in the cut, like I told your ass," when the word "ass" is lowered to the point that a very distinct croaky quality occurs. This is also done on Scarface's "Hand of the Dead Body" (00:44) when he raps, "So gangsta rap ain't done shit for that," and lowers the pitch on the word "that" to the point that it is said with a croaky quality.

Sometimes this kind of sound can be added without thinking about it—especially if the MC has an unpredictable vocal style to begin with.

RBX

I don't really be trying to make it crazy, that's pretty much just the mood I'm in at the time, and my voice just does [unpredictable things]. I don't have no real major, major voice control, I just got a voice that just [does that]. When I'm in the mode and I'm doing my thing and it comes out the way it comes out, sometimes I can't even do it again, like, "Whoa, we're gonna leave it like that!" And just hopefully I can learn it in time for when I do it live.

Changing Pitch on a Syllable or Word

As well as changing the pitch of a syllable so that it's at a different pitch to the syllables around it, you can also change the pitch *on* the syllable, so that the pitch goes from high to low or from low to high on just that one syllable.

High to Low Pitch on a Syllable or Word

An example of when the pitch of a single sound goes from high to low in pitch is on Organized Konfusion's "Drop Bombs" (00:10) with the opening lyrics, "Organized drop bombs," with the pitch on the word "bombs" going from high to low—this also mimics the sound of a bomb being dropped.

Low to High Pitch on a Word

Alternatively, the pitch on a syllable can go from low to high— the very beginning of Fu-Schnickens's "Breakdown" (00:01) has "breakdown" being said with the pitch on the syllable "down" going from low to high pitch.

Tech N9ne

If I say, "I seen her last night," [going up in pitch on "seen"], if I don't say [it in the same way] on my Dictaphone, the next morning I might say, "I seen her last night," [with the pitch going down on "seen"], it won't be the same thing, so I gotta put it on my recorder. I put it on my Dictaphone, so I keep that pitch.

Up and Down Pitch on a Syllable or Word

The pitch on a syllable can also go up and down repeatedly—this can be used as a type of *vibrato* that we will look at later (p. 122).

This is done on Snoop Dogg's "Tha Shiznit" (01:54) near the middle of the song, with the lyrics "Yooou caaan't see." The words "you" and "can't" have a fluctuating pitch to them that wobbles up and down. Similarly, on Fu-Schnickens's "Visions (20-20)" (01:44) the phrase "Metamorphasiiiize and visions twenty, twenty, right in

front of your eeeeyes" has up and down pitch on the syllable "size"
and the word "eyes."

Changing the Pitch on a Whole Phrase

Rather than changing pitch on just a single syllable or word, the
pitch can be changed over the course of a whole phrase (where a
"phrase" can be anything from a few words to a whole sentence; a
bar of music or even several bars of music).

Variety

As with raising and lowering pitch on a syllable, one of the main
uses of these techniques is to add variety. Examples of this include
Q-Tip on A Tribe Called Quest's "If the Papes Come" (02:04) when
the phrase "Get me a spliff" is raised gradually in pitch from low
to high, and RBX on Snoop Dogg's "Serial Killa" (02:40) with the
phrase "Open and release them guts," which goes from high to
low pitch smoothly—both use these techniques to add variety and
interest to the delivery.

R.A. the Rugged Man
50 [Cent], you listen to some of his stuff and he'll go and
change the [pitch] here and there, and you'll go, "Oh, he's
changing this up." A record like "Window Shopper," he's
doing that high pitched and low pitched and changing this
and that—he changes it up.

Lower to Higher Pitch on a Phrase

The pitch can be raised from a lower pitch to a higher pitch over
the course of a phrase. This has many of the same effects as raising

the pitch on a single syllable, though it raises the pitch gradually, rather than raising it sharply on one sound.

Gradual Sense of Urgency

The gradual raising of pitch over a series of syllables can make this technique more suspenseful than raising it only on a single syllable and can give a creeping sense of urgency as the vocal gets higher over a longer time. This is done by E-40 on the track "Growing Up" (01:30) on the phrase near the middle of the track, "I don't think I'll make it to see twenty-five," which goes from lower to higher pitch gradually over the length of the phrase and creates a building sense of urgency that matches the subject matter.

Opening a Verse

An effective way to start the first line of a verse is to raise the pitch from low to high on that line—this gives a kind of "sliding into the verse" effect, as the pitch comes up smoothly. Rakim does this on Eric B. & Rakim's "In the Ghetto" (01:38) on the verse beginning "I learned to relax." This opening line rises in pitch over a series of syllables, launching smoothly into the verse.

Guerilla Black

If it ain't got no swagger on it [with variation in the delivery, then] it was just ok—you pulled off a real clever punch line [but it could have been better]. I look at everything as "tricks" you pulled off—it's your presence in your way that you pull off your tricks that's gonna make the difference. Your swagger, the way you pull off the trick, that's what makes it even hotter. If you just pull off a crazy trick and it was stiff, it was like, "Oh, he pulled off a crazy trick, but it was all right . . . it was great, but it wasn't fantastic."

Higher to Lower Pitch on a Phrase

Pitch can be lowered from a high pitch to a lower pitch over a line. Again, this has some similar effects to the lowering of pitch on a particular syllable, but it is more gradual and so the technique can often have a smoother effect.

Strong Statement with Seriousness

Going from higher to lower pitch over a line can give it a strong sense of seriousness. This is good for statements in which you want to make a point.

Scarface does this a lot in his delivery, which gives his songs a very strong sense of someone who is serious about his content and who is telling you something important. For example, on his song "Hand of the Dead Body" (00:40), lines such as "Gangsta NIP, Spice 1, and 2Pac never gave a gun to me" are said while going from higher to lower pitch over the course of the line, giving it extra weight and importance.

Gift of Gab of Blackalicious does this on many lines on the song "Swan Lake" (01:12) and again, this results in a sense of seriousness and solemnity throughout the song.

MC Shan

That's where the recorder comes in, because you can write down a rhyme and have the style in your head that night, go back tomorrow and be like, "[Damn], how was I saying it?" You know what you're saying, but the style is not [the same], it ain't the same as when you thought about it.

Ending a Verse

Just as opening a verse can work well using low-to-high pitch, ending a verse with a line going from high to low pitch can be effective, as it smoothly brings a feeling of finality to the end of the verse. This is done on Snoop Dogg's "Murder Was the Case" (01:27), when the first verse ends with "My eyes are closed," moving from a higher to a lower pitch to finish the verse.

Whole Phrases at Different Pitches

As well as certain syllables changing pitch and certain lines changing from one pitch to another gradually, whole lines can simply be raised or lowered in pitch as a whole unit—the first line could all be at a low pitch, followed by the second line all at a higher pitch, and the whole third line could then be at a lower pitch, and so on. For example, Snoop Dogg's "Murder Was the Case" (01:15) has the phrase "How long will I live?" and the whole phrase is raised in pitch compared to the lyrics surrounding it.

Shock G, Digital Underground

[The end of "Humpty Dance" (04:25) when the whole line goes up in pitch compared to the previous lines,] that came spontaneously, just trying to keep up with the progressive energy of the samples as it kicked into overdrive . . . "GIMME DA MUZIICCK!"

Creating Patterns with Pitch

Often, series of lower- and higher-pitched syllables or phrases will be used to create a pattern in the delivery. This can be done to create a structure for the verse, in a similar way to how rhythm or rhyme is sometimes used. This happens on Tone-Lōc's "Wild Thing" (01:20):

Shopping at the mall, [*lower pitch*]
Looking for some gear to buy, [*higher pitch*]

I saw this girl, she cold rocked my world, [*steady pitch*]
And I had to adjust my fly. [*lower pitch*]

He ends the first line by lowering the pitch on the word "mall,"
then the second line ends with a rise in pitch on the word "buy."
The third line stays at a steady pitch with no obvious change, and
then the fourth line ends with a lower pitch on the word "fly."

Phife Dawg of A Tribe Called Quest creates a pattern on his
verse on Fu-Schnickens's "La Schmoove" (02:30):

Get on the board, lay down the tracks and I'll do ten laps,
   [*steady pitch*]
Pass the pen, pass the pad, and I'll kick 'nough raps, [*steady
   pitch*]
Just come inside your jam and witness who is boss, [*higher
   pitch*]
And it won't be Tony Danza nor Diana Ross. [*lower pitch*]

The first two lines have relatively steady pitches, then the third
line ends with a higher pitch on the word "boss" and the fourth
line ends with a lower pitch on the word "Ross." This four-line
pattern repeats throughout a lot of Phife Dawg's verse and sets a
structure using pitch in the delivery.

Part of Spice 1's track "RIP" (02:12) also creates a pattern with
the pitch:

My nigga had bomb, [*lower pitch*]
We called him Big Dave, [*higher pitch*]
Six slugs in the chest [*steady pitch*]
Put my boy in the grave. [*lower pitch*]

The lines go from first ending with a lower pitch, then a higher
pitch, then a steady pitch, then finishing with a lower pitch. These
types of patterns are also done with melody in half-sung rapping,
which we will look at later (p. 145).

Although these patterns may sometimes seem more rudimentary, they can be a very effective way to successfully complement the music.

Thes One, People Under the Stairs

All of the people we knew that were strictly MCs, they looked at their rhymes as being a 100 percent focus of the song, [but] we looked at it more so as a song being 50 percent the rhyme and 50 percent the beat, [so] we had a hard time dealing with cats rhyming over our beats. To harness that [MCing] energy and make it a song is difficult—I kind of feel like there has been a lot of great rhymers, but the dudes could never make songs or albums. There's been a lot of great freestylers, they can just sit and rhyme and rhyme and rhyme, but they can't make [good] music [if they don't complement the beat].

Stretching and Shortening Sounds

One aspect of delivery that is not often discussed but can make a huge difference to the overall sound is the stretching of certain words and the shortening of words (this shortening is sometimes known as a "staccato" delivery).

Stretching Sounds

Stretching certain sounds is a technique used by a large number of MCs. It is generally used on a few words or syllables in a verse, rather than for each and every syllable—this makes its use different from the shortening of sounds, as shortening tends to be used for whole lines and even whole verses.

A lot of MCs have a specific symbol they write down on paper to let them know which words to stretch out in the delivery.

Bootie Brown, The Pharcyde

I have these different little symbols to say, OK, hold this note longer or shift this word.

To Put Emphasis on a Word

The most common use of stretching out a sound is to put more emphasis on a particular word, as it gives the word more prominence and lets the word take up more time than the other words. 2Pac did this a lot in his delivery, such as on the tracks "Breathin'" (00:24) ("Enemiiies give me reeeason") and "So Many Tears" (00:27) ("Until I got that thuuuug life tattooed on my chest, tell me, can you feeeeel me?"). This is another example of a technique that can really be put to good use once the lyrics are memorized, as you are then able to put more thought into the delivery, even if you didn't do so initially.

Pusha-T, Clipse

When you have it memorized, that's when you begin to finesse and play with the verse, that's when you get to throw your voice and that's when you get to get more arrogant and cocky saying your verse, or put emphasis on something. Because you know the words, now it's just conveying it.

As a Change in Rhythm

When a sound is stretched, it often affects the rhythm of the lyrics, as one sound now takes up more space than it would if it were said normally, and if the sound is stretched out long enough, it pushes the rest of the lyrics further back.

This isn't done too often or to a large degree in rapping, as most of the focus is on shorter, percussive rhythmic sounds, rather than long, drawn-out sounds (drawn-out sounds are done far more in singing), but it is done occasionally, just to help break up the rhythm and make it more varied.

An example of when a single sound is held for a long time, taking up space where other syllables would have been and pushing the rest of the lyrics back, is by Ol' Dirty Bastard on Wu-Tang Clan's "Da Mystery of Chessboxin'" (02:32) when he says, "Ghost- . . . face . . . Killlllaaaaaaah."

If we put this into a flow diagram, we can see that the "no one can get iller" part could have been said on the second bar, but by stretching the "killah" part of the lyrics, the "no one can get iller" part is pushed way back onto the third bar, altering the rhythm of the verse and the placement of the words:

1	2	3	4
Intro-	ducing the	Ghost-	face
Killaaaaaaaaaaaaaaaaaaaaaaaaaaaaaaaaaaaaaaaaaaaaaaaaaaaaaaaaaaaaaaaaaaaaaaa-			
aaaaaaaaaaaaaaaaaaaaaaaaaaaaaaaaaah.	No one can get		iller.

Another example is on Organized Konfusion's "Drop Bombs" (00:09), which we can see here in a flow diagram:

1	2	3	4
			Orga-
nized drop	booooooooooooooooooooooooooooooooooooooo-		
ooombs.	Guer- rilla war-	fare like Viet-	nam.

And again, the long syllable (the word "bombs") pushes back the next phrase ("Guerrilla warfare like Vietnam"), giving it a different rhythm than if that syllable wasn't stretched.

A syllable doesn't have to be stretched as far as these examples for it have a rhythmic impact—even stretching out a syllable a little bit means it can take the place where another syllable could have been.

For Variety in the Delivery

As well as altering the rhythm, stretching syllables also makes words sound different, and therefore it allows for more variety

Stretching and Shortening Sounds

Stretching and Shortening Sounds   **III**

in the delivery. Adding some stretched syllables can break up a verse that is being said in mostly shorter sounds and makes it more varied and interesting to listen to. On Snoop Dogg's "Murder Was the Case" (01:50), he includes several longer syllables, such as in the phrases "To get back on my *feeeet*," and "Came to *realityyyyy*," in which the syllables "feet" and "-ty" are stretched.

Guerilla Black

It's like if I say, "I got my gun," or I say, "I gooot my guuuun" [*stretching the sounds*]. You'd remember the second way more than you'd remember the first way, because of the swagger that I put on the word.

Adding Personality

Stretching the length of certain words can become part of someone's style and can add a lot of personality. For example, Snoop Dogg has a couple of phrases with stretched syllables—these are "you knooow" (in which "knooow" is stretched) and "beeeaatch" (in which the word "bitch" is stretched out into two syllables, "beee-" and "-aatch"). 2Pac's stretching of syllables also added a lot of character to his delivery, as there were certain words he would often stretch ("enemiiiies" and "Hennesseeeeey," for example).

One Be Lo, Binary Star

I'm real picky about how I say certain things, [and] only I know how I want to say it. So if I'm in the booth and everybody's like, "That shit sounds great," but I don't like the way I said one word, I'm just gonna re-spit the whole verse. I could say, "The greatest of all time," or I could say, "The greatest of all tiiiiiiime," and to me it's something totally different, because once it's recorded, people are gonna remember that you said that word exactly that way forever.

Stretching a Sound to Start a Verse

An effective way to go into a new verse is to draw out the first word or syllable of the verse, to launch into it. The Beastie Boys employ this technique a lot, on tracks such as "Intergalactic" (01:46) ("Nooooow, when it comes to envy, y'all is green"), "Alive" (02:23) ("Nooooow, I'ma break it down to the brass tacks"), and "Remote Control" (00:11) ("Weeeeell, things get hectic quick").

Stretching a Sound to End a Verse

Stretching out the last syllable of a verse as a way to end it can be an effective technique, as it lets the final sound linger and stay in the listener's head. This is done on Snoop Dogg's song "G Funk Intro" (01:35)—he ends one of his half-sung sections saying, ". . . with the D, R, Eeeee" and the letter *e* is stretched. It is also used on the Beastie Boys' "So What'cha Want" (00:53), with the lyrics before the chorus: "When revelation coooomes. . . ."

Aesop Rock

I have this shorthand that I've just kind of developed over the course of the last [few] years—symbols of where the end of four bars is [and] if I need to drag a word out, there's a little symbol for that.

Shortening Sounds (Staccato Delivery)

In contrast to lengthening certain sounds, sounds can also be shortened—syllables can be said in short bursts, and this creates a different type of sound from lengthening. In music, this is known as a staccato delivery, and it has what can be called a "choppy," "crisp," or "abrupt" sound, as the sounds are shorter and clipped. It has the effect of clearly separating the sounds, so that each individual syllable is more clear-cut and crisp.

Shortening Sounds to Enhance the Rhythm

Shortening sounds makes the delivery more "choppy," so you can really hear the precise hits of the syllables against the beat. Because you're shortening each syllable, there is more room to play with the syncopation (syncopation is explained in the first *How to Rap*, p. 256—it's when lyrics are said slightly behind or ahead of the music's beat). The more staccato the delivery, the closer the MC will sound to percussion, as a lot of percussion instruments are staccato sounding—they use sharp, short drum hits, rather than longer sounds.

Stat Quo

It's all about the beat—the snare, the hi-hat. I just follow the drums and I try to make my voice be an instrument as the drums are.

This is particularly useful when performing raps that have a lot of 16ths, 32nds, and fast triplets (as described in chapter 1 of this book), as you can make all the individual syllables hit with real precision if they're made shorter—the Lady of Rage's track "Get with Da Wickedness" (00:01) is an example in which rhythms with 16ths are enhanced by a staccato delivery.

Del the Funky Homosapien says he will sometimes shorten sounds to get them to sound like percussion. "Matter of fact, I've studied drumming, so I know percussively what I'm doing."

Shortening Sounds to Split Up Words

Making each syllable shorter and separating each of them has the effect of splitting up words into their individual sounds in a really clear way—this is used quite a lot by certain MCs for making particular words sound more interesting, or simply just different from how they sound normally.

LL Cool J does this on the track "Around the Way Girl" (01:27) when he raps, "You can break hearts and ma-nip-u-late minds," splitting the word "manipulate" into clear-cut syllables to make the word sound distinct.

Shortening Sounds as Part of an Effect

Shortening sounds can be used in combination with other techniques to create certain overall effects. For example, on Latyrx's track "Latyrx" (02:36) Lyrics Born's verse, which begins, "Now that we have made our way away from the . . ." is said using a staccato delivery combined with changes in pitch and accent that come together to give the delivery an interesting sound, sort of like an android rapping.

Aesop Rock

Once you get a grip on using words and what you can do with them and what you can do with your own voice, you start trying things. A verse is short enough to experiment, and if it doesn't work you don't have to ever do it again.

Shortening Sounds for Clarity and Precision

Fast raps that require a lot of syllables to be said clearly usually require a staccato style of delivery, so that the words can be more easily comprehended. Fast-rapping MCs such as Tech N9ne use this technique—his track "Welcome to the Midwest" (00:08) uses a lot of staccato in the first verse to make sure the lyrics are said clearly and precisely. Writing to the specific beat that will be rapped over often helps MCs judge how long or short syllables should be.

Evidence, Dilated Peoples

I used to do that a lot, just write without a beat, [but] then I had a problem where I would start squeezing words in sometimes or have a lack of words and extending certain words that shouldn't have been extended. So I kinda figured it's always better for me to try to script my lyrics to a track.

Stuttering and Repetition

A couple of popular techniques that can be used in a variety of situations are stuttering and repetition. These are particularly useful in adding more rhythmic elements to a verse.

Stuttering

Stuttering is when a particular sound is repeated, usually quite quickly. This differs from more straightforward repetition, in which usually a whole word is repeated. An example of stuttering with the word "fresh" would be when the "f" sound at the beginning of the word is repeated several times before saying the full word—"f-f-f-f-fresh."

Andy Cat, Ugly Duckling

[Stuttering] seems to have worked in a lot of songs from many different genres—[for example,] "Stuttering Blues" by John Lee Hooker, "My Generation" by the Who, and "You Ain't Seen Nothin' Yet" by Bachman-Turner Overdrive. I think any decent songwriter and/or vocalist is always looking for an interesting and impactful way to reach a listener. In my opinion, it would be unwise to rely too much on these kinds of things, but the stutter is certainly a tool to have in the belt.

Stuttering to Mimic an Actual Stutter

The most obvious use of stuttering is to mimic an actual stutter, when someone can't get his or her words out and keeps repeating the first sound. One of the most elaborate examples of this is when the idea of becoming nervous and developing a stutter is mentioned in both the content and in the delivery, through actual stuttering, in DJ Jazzy Jeff & the Fresh Prince's "Boom! Shake the Room" (02:34). The Fresh Prince raps with a stutter throughout the first half of the whole third verse, at the same time rapping about the stutter: "But sometimes I get n-nervous and start to stutter, and I f-fumble every w-w-word I utter, so I just try to ch-ch-ch-ch-ch-chill. . . ."

One of the most memorable lines in Big Daddy Kane's "Set It Off" (00:38) also includes a stutter, when he raps, "E-E-E-Even if I stutter, I will still come off." This not only allows him to suggest how good an MC he is, that he can rap even when stuttering, but it also lets him actually demonstrate it by doing it in the delivery.

Stuttering to Open a New Verse

A popular use of stuttering is to stutter the first sound of the first word of a verse before the verse begins, as a type of introduction to launch into it. It lets the listener know that a verse is about to begin and adds the equivalent of a little rhythmic drum roll to give the MC momentum before coming in strong with the verse.

This is used on Stop the Violence Movement's "Self Destruction" (02:07), in which one of the verses begins, "St-St-St-Straight from the mouth . . .," as well as before the first verse of the Beatnuts' track "Third of the Trio" (00:30).

Stuttering for Rhythmic Variety

Stuttering can be added one or more times in a song simply to provide more variety to the rhythm and sound of the track. Beatnuts' "Third of the Trio" (01:45, 00:42, and 00:51) has several examples of this throughout ("I'm not a crimin-imin-al," "d-d-d deep," "styles so s-sweet," "b-b-butter baby") and the Pharcyde's "Ya Mama" (02:27) does this during one of the choruses ("I . . . I, I, I said, ya mama's got a peg-leg with a kickstand").

A stuttered word or sound may be the result of a mistake while recording. It may be kept in because it adds to the rhythm, even if it wasn't planned beforehand.

MURS

9th Wonder, my producer, he never allows me to do stuff over, he's all about the feeling in the moment—if I stuttered a word, he doesn't care, as long as I make it through. [So the] first take I get all the way through, I usually just leave it.

Stuttering as an Impressive Technique

Sometimes a stutter is used to show the skill of the MC, as it takes great enunciation to get a stuttered verse out clearly and to get the same sounds out in different rhythms with lots of extra syllables.

A great example of this is on Organized Konfusion's "Bring It On" (01:02) when Pharoahe Monch raps, "I am s-s-selecting, n-n-n-n-new styles, for p-p-p-p-piles piles of MCs who try to get b-b-b-buck buckwild, f-f-f-fuck that!" Here, several stuttering sounds are used in a short space of time, really highlighting the ability of the MC to deliver difficult raps.

Eminem also does this sort of fast-paced stuttering on Bad Meets Evil's "Fast Lane" (02:25) when he raps, "Little t-t-trailer trash, take a look who's back in t-t-town, did I st-st-stutter, mother-fucker? Fuck them all, he shuts a whole motherfucking Walmart d-d-down every time he comes a-r-r-round."

However, adding difficult parts to a song in this way can often make it hard to perform live, as you are not able to do several takes to get it right.

El Da Sensei

You also gotta remember when you finish doing that song, you gonna have to do it on stage, so you gotta make sure that you're not going too crazy. You can be action packed throughout the whole song and forget that you gonna be doing it on stage: you think you're in the booth again. There ain't no take one, take two—now you're just up there and you gotta [perform it in one go].

Stuttering as Part of a Vocal Trademark

A stutter can be part of a vocal trademark (see "Vocal Trademark Sound or Phrase," p. 137), as it can be a distinct way of saying something that will stick with the listener. 50 Cent's G-Unit uses this as their way of stamping their mark on the track, by saying, "G-G-G-G-unit" on tracks such as "Eye for Eye" (00:10) and "G-Unit" (00:18). RZA's "The Whistle" (00:12) uses a similar technique, with him starting the track with "di-di-di-di-di-digital."

Alternate Stutter Technique

An alternate stutter technique can be done, in which the first sound of a word is said, then an "a" sound in the middle, and then the actual word. So for example, if the word in the rap was "popped," it would become "puh-a-popped."

An extensive example of this is on Spice 1's "I'm the Fuckin' Murderer" (01:19) during the second and third verses, with lines such as, "I roll down the ruh-a-road, down the buh-a-block, hand on the huh-a-hand on the guh-a-glock." Spice 1 uses the same technique on the tracks "The Murda Show" (02:59) ("tuh-a, tuh-a, tech") and "Mo' Mal" (02:41) ("thu-a, thu-a throat," "ru-a-ratta, tu-a-tatta"). E-40 has also used this technique on "Record Haters" (03:25) ("all about my ru-a-rap, shu-a-shrine") and "Million Dollar Spot" (00:48) ("a buh-a bucket").

Stuttering can be combined with other techniques, such as exhaling on a word (looked at further on p. 135), as on E-40's song, "Growing Up" (02:39) toward the end of the last verse ("a sme-*ah*, a smeb-rover," where "ah" is exhaled loudly in the middle of the stuttering technique).

Repetition

Regular repetition is when a whole word or phrase is repeated, which can be done for several reasons and to create different effects.

Repeating Words in a Particular Rhythm

As seen in chapter 1, when using techniques such as triplets, the same words are often repeated (p. 21). This is usually done to emphasize the rhythmic technique and put it center stage in the verse—the listener knows that the content is simply the same word over and over, and this draws more attention to the rhythm being used. This is done on Fu-Schnickens's "What's Up Doc?" (01:10) with the repeated word "Figaro, Figaro, Figaro, Figaro."

Repeating Words to Combine Content and Rhythm

KRS-One's "Sound of Da Police" (01:36) uses repetition to emphasize both the content *and* the rhythm at the same time. This is during the part of the song when he raps, "Take the word overseer" and then "repeat it very quickly," which leads to the repetition in which he raps, "Overseer . . . overseer . . . overseer . . . overseer . . . officer-officer-officer-officer."

The highlighted part in the previous example shows where the word is repeated fast enough that it blurs between sounding like "overseer" and "officer," which is the point of the line—he is saying that there are big similarities between overseers and officers, and he uses repetition and a fast rhythm to get this message across in the delivery as well as the content.

Repeating Words Throughout a Verse or Song

Sometimes repetition can be used throughout a verse or song to make it more distinct. For example, Lateef on Latyrx's song

"Latyrx" (03:48) performs a verse in which the final word of most of the lines is repeated:

> More and more suckas getting signed for less, less, less, and less,
> And lesson one, if aiming to impress, press, press . . .

The Ultramagnetic MCs' track "One, Two, One, Two" (00:19) has a similar structure, repeating certain words twice:

> Over and switch, switch, change my pitch, pitch,
> You can get down, down, rock with my sound, sound . . .

This type of repetition throughout a track can come as a result of fitting the lyrics to a particular beat in an interesting way, or to mimic part of a drum pattern.

Esoteric

On [the track] "Daisycutta," I completely formatted the words to fit with the drum pattern, almost to the point where I let the drums choose the words for me—I kept repeating the second to last word of each line to match with the drums.

Repetition for Rhythmic Variety

Saying the same word again, instead of immediately going into the next line of the lyrics, changes the rhythm, as it adds more syllables and pushes the rest of the lyrics back. For example, André 3000 on OutKast's "Gangsta Shit" (03:49) raps, "Pop-pop, lock-lock, to-the, to-the beat-beat." By repeating the words "pop," "lock," "beat," and the phrase "to the," he alters the rhythm by adding many more syllables than if he simply rapped, "Pop, lock, to the beat" without the repetition.

One-off instances of repetition can also be used to heighten a specific part of the music, particularly when the repetition closely follows a section of the rhythm in the track.

Andy Cat, Ugly Duckling

With [the track] "Slow the Flow" (01:56) [where I say, "Fast, fast, fast, fast"], I planned that one out to work with the drum fill, which brings the track from half-time [tempo] back to the main tempo, and I was really pleased with the result. That's one of those things that really works best when recorded on two tracks—you can record yourself right up against another one of your vocals to get that tight, percussive power and pan them [with one vocal in the right speaker and one in the left] to make it feel big; like a stereo drum solo where the listener is getting hit from all directions. I really like the Rick James song "Mary Jane" when the bridge goes, "Do ya, do ya, do ya, do ya. . . ." It has that feel.

To Address Someone and for Emphasis

Sometimes a name or phrase will be repeated if it's meant to address someone or to emphasize a particular part of the content. On Slick Rick's "La Di Da Di" (04:00, on the unedited version) he raps, "Ricky, Ricky, Ricky, can't you see," and the Pharcyde's "Passin' Me By" (03:35) includes the line "My dear, my dear, my dear." Both of these are examples of the MC referring to someone and using repetition to make that reference clearer.

Snoop Dogg's "Who Am I (What's My Name)?" (00:34) has the line "Follow me, follow me, follow me, follow me," in which he emphasizes through repetition exactly what he wants the listener to do.

Vibrato

Vibrato is used in most forms of music, and it is used in a similar way in rapping. It is a pulsating effect made by quickly and repeatedly changing pitch or volume. It creates a shaking or wobbling sound, like the voice is "vibrating."

This can be heard on Snoop Dogg's song "Serial Killa" (02:18) during the chorus section after Snoop Dogg's verse, in which the lyrics are "Serial killa-a-a-a-aahhh." The word "killer" has vibrato on the second part of it, where the sound fluctuates with the amount of breath the MC is using to say the sound. Fu-Schnickens's track "Breakdown" (01:30) has vibrato at the ends of the sneezes that are done—a sort of gurgling vibrato sound is made, and the Fugees' song "Cowboys" (00:10) uses vibrato during the chorus ("Oh-lay-*heeee*," where the "heeee" part has vibrato on it).

Pharoahe Monch uses vibrato on several tracks, such as on Organized Konfusion's "Thirteen" (02:44) ("*Laaa*-di-da," where he makes the "laaa" vibrate) and "Black Sunday" (00:08, 01:31, and 01:41) ("*Noooo* matter the weather," on the "noooo," and "*Loooord*, help us to," on the "Loooord," and "Crack *viiiials*," on the "viiii-als"). It is sometimes also used for an atmospheric, eerie vibe, as on the end of Tha Dogg Pound's "Dogg Pound 4 Life" (04:16), where there is some vibrato present. Recording the vocal to hear yourself creating the sound can help to perfect it.

Vinnie Paz, Jedi Mind Tricks

I think that the way that you hone your skills is to [record]. Stoupe and I were making tapes and recording songs for years before we'd even let people hear them, and that's how you get better, you have to record. I know people who are really dope and then they get into a studio and sound like shit. So I think you need to record, even if it's on a shitty mic or other people's beats. That's how you get better.

Bootie Brown, The Pharcyde

Sometimes I just want to hear it on a tape, I wanna hear

myself, how I'm coming off. So I just want to record it so I can say, "OK this is what I want to work on."

Section C | Sounds Without Words

Scatting and Random Rhythmic Sounds

In the first *How to Rap*, p. 114, we saw how scatting can be a great way for an MC to come up with rhythms, later replacing the random sounds with actual words. However, scatting can be used as a technique in its own right, for when you might want a section without words at all—for variety and to make the track more entertaining.

Lateef, Latyrx

Study songs and styles, widen your range of listening—listen for rap in places that you might not expect it. Listen for rap and styles in places like in reggae or in jazz scatting or in other genres of music. Listen to the style versus the genre, because I've heard country songs that sound like they're rapping.

Lord Jamar, Brand Nubian

I can give you flows all day with no words to it, we call that scatting. Me and my friends, we scat rhymes out sometimes, you get ideas.

One Sound Repeated

Scatting can be done by taking one sound, such as "laa" or "naa," and repeating that one sound in a rhythm or series of rhythms. Examples of this include the D.O.C. on his track "Funky Enough" (00:46) ("naa naa naa na-na-na-na"), on Cypress Hill's "Hand on the Pump" (01:04) ("la-la la-la, la-laa, laa, laaaaa"), and on Organized Konfusion's "Let's Organize" (02:09) ("laalaalaalaalaaaa").

Variations Around One Sound

Possibly the most popular form of scatting vocals is to take one general sound, such as a "b" sound, an "m" sound, or a "d" sound, and then join a variety of other sounds to this main sound.

Boogie Down Productions' "9mm Goes Bang" (00:54) uses the phrase "wah dah-dar dang, wah dah-da-dar dang." The main sound that is repeated is a "d" sound, but it is used as part of slightly different sounds, "dah," "dar," "dang," and "da." "Wah" is used to break up the "d" sounds as well.

Other phrases and songs that use this form of scatting include Boogie Down Productions' "The Bridge Is Over" (01:21) ("di-di-di-dah, di-di-di, di-di-da-di day"), Snoop Dogg's "Pump, Pump" (02:16) ("dee dee-dee-dadi daa, blah, bidda-baa, ba-bom, ba-bom"), De La Soul's "Buddy (Native Tongues Decision Mix)" (00:19) ("minna-minna-minna-minnaaa"), Melle Mel on Grandmaster Flash and the Furious Five's "The Message" (01:29) ("uh-huh huh huh"), and Busta Rhymes on A Tribe Called Quest's "Scenario" (03:17) ("uh, uuuh-uh, all over the track").

Lateef, Latyrx

I always recommend young MCs to listen to Lambert, Hendricks & Ross, they did a lot of jazz scatting stuff. They had a song called "Cloudburst" that's light years ahead of a lot of the stuff a lot of MCs are doing now. That was in the '50s, and that shit is as good or better than most cats are rapping right now, probably better.

Yells and Shouts

Yells and shouts can be done in rhythms, and this creates another type of scatting with a different type of sound. This is done on De La Soul's track "Ego Trippin' (Part Two)" (00:15), which begins with rhythmic yells, as well as on Organized Konfusion's "Drop Bombs" (00:06), which also starts with rhythmic yells and "aaarghs."

Made-Up or Altered Words

Sometimes random sounds can be made by altering words so that they no longer have any meaning—this is done in some children's games, such as "The Name Game." Tim Dog's "I Get Wrecked" (04:32) and Eminem's lyrics on D12's "Git Up" (00:33) both use "The Name Game" to create nonsensical lyrics in this way (Tim Dog raps, "Doggy boggy bo boggy, banana fana fo foggy, me mi mo moggy, doggy," and Eminem raps, "Banana fana fo fanas"). Heltah Skeltah also make up words to fit into a rhythm for the intro and title of their track "Leflaur Leflah Eshkoshka" (00:06).

Del the Funky Homosapien
With [the song] "Slam Dunk" I think I actually did write on the paper, "Skibbidy doo-dah-day." I think I did actually write that down. It was planned out—I knew I was gonna say that there. But nowadays, I freestyle a lot of my lyrics, so it allows me to add little stuff like that, more than writing, because writing, I'm more serious, I'm more directed, I'm more looking at the page and how the words connect, which doesn't always translate well into hearing.

Vocal Sound Effects and Beatboxing

Vocal Sound Effects

Vocal sound effects and mimicking a variety of sounds are good ways to make vocals more interesting and have been used on a lot of classic tracks by a variety of MCs.

By knowing the sorts of creative and interesting vocal sound effects that have been done before, you can draw from a range of already-established techniques to use in your delivery, as well as being able to tell whether you are innovating or using a technique that has already been employed.

Brother Ali

I think that a lot of MCs are cheating themselves by not tapping into this great legacy of music that we have, that we're a part of. If you feel a kinship to what came before in hip-hop or feel like that's where we're getting what we're doing now, and feel a connection to it, then it's kind of a platform you stand on, and it strengthens you as an artist. To say, "All these things came before me and they're making me who I am and I have the power of all of that behind what I'm saying," it can really strengthen you. I feel like a lot of people don't have that, and they kind of pop out of the woodwork and they're not connected to anything and you can hear it.

Gunshots

One of the most commonly mimicked sounds are gunshot sounds. These are done in a number of different ways.

Some of the most popular ways of mimicking gunshot sounds are: "biddy-bom-bom!" on Dr. Dre's "Day the Niggaz Took Over" (02:05); "blaaa!" on Spice 1's "Smoke 'Em Like A Blunt" (00:10), "The Murda Show" (03:38), and "Trigga Gots No Heart" (02:43); "bleuw, bleuw!" on Spice 1's "Mo' Mal" (03:09); "buck!" on Brotha Lynch Hung's "Season of Da Sicc" (01:42) and "Welcome 2 Your Own Death" (01:41); "pap, pap" and "pop" on "Season of Da Sicc" (00:23 and 00:36); "rat-a-tat-tat" on Organized Konfusion's "Stray Bullet" (01:36) and Dr. Dre's "Rat a Tat Tat" (00:36); "ch-ch-baow!" on Wu-Tang Clan's "C.R.E.A.M." (01:28); "blaaow!" by Method Man on 2Pac's "Got My Mind Made Up" (03:26); "bam, bam!" and "baka, baka, baka!" on Notorious B.I.G.'s "Gimme the Loot"

(03:53 and 03:07); and "brrdddiya!" on MC Eiht's "Represent" (00:22).

Andy Cat, Ugly Duckling

I think of all those things as "flavor." When Einstein [Ugly Duckling's producer] and I are producing the music, the final phase we go through is what we call "bells and whistles." We add things like sound effects, scratches, hits, drum fills [etc.] and, hopefully, all of this puts a little more charge in the ideas we're trying to get across. Obviously, you could go too far with this and have these things become a distraction, so we're always trying to strike that balance the way that [Public Enemy's producers] the Bomb Squad and Dr. Dre did in [their classic tracks].

Animals

Animal noises are sometimes mimicked by MCs. These include chicken noises, such as "pa-cccaawk!" on Cypress Hill's "3 Lil' Putos" (02:36); bird noises like "haaw-haaw!" on Organized Konfusion's "Why" (02:08) and "aaayaah, aaayaah!" on Ice Cube's "Ghetto Bird" (00:01) and Xzibit on Snoop Dogg's "Bitch Please" (00:15); dog noises such as "ggggrrrrrah!" on Organized Konfusion's "3-2-1" (01:04) and barking noises on DMX's "The Omen" (01:02); and bee noises like "bbzzzz-bbzzzz" on Chino XL's "No Complex" (01:59).

Sometimes sounds like these can be worked into the content in clever ways, such as in the Lady of Rage's "Unfucwitable" (01:30) when she raps, "I stay wide-eyed like an owl, now *hoo-hoo* flows better than this rhyme writer." Here, the "hoo-hoo" part is said mimicking an owl, highlighting the owl reference just before it, but it also sounds like "who-who," as she is also asking "Who flows better than this rhyme writer?"

Including these kinds of vocal effects can add to the variety of the delivery, but some MCs warn that a track can become overcrowded if you use too many.

Del the Funky Homosapien

If you start adding too much, it starts to become congested, and you can't make out anything that's in the mix, because stuff starts masking each other. It's confusing after a while—you start getting mud—so taking shit away is actually very valid. You hear people say "Less is more" . . . It is! Because you get to hear more of what's going on—[sometimes] when you add more you're starting to take away from the experience, because it's too much for you to digest at once.

Vinyl Scratching

The sound of a DJ scratching a vinyl record can be mimicked, such as by Eminem on Dr. Dre's "Forgot About Dre" (02:01) ("Chicka-chicka-chicka, Slim Shady, hotter than . . .") and by Rahzel on the chorus to Rakim's "It's a Must" (01:03) and on his own track "All I Know" (00:21 and 00:50), in which he also mimics a record being rewound quickly.

Other Noises

A lot of other sounds can be imitated on records—this often happens when there is a reference in the content that would benefit from a vocal sound effect to bring the content to life. This includes imitating police sirens, as with KRS-One's "whoop-whoop!" on "Sound of Da Police" (00:01); tires screeching as on Organized Konfusion's "Thirteen" (00:23); video game sound effects as on the Lady of Rage's "Afro Puffs" (01:19), which includes her saying "haayooken!" a sound from the game *Street Fighter 2*; and the sound of a chainsaw, as done by Chino XL on "Deliver" (02:49) and Eminem on "Kill You" (00:53).

Andy Cat, Ugly Duckling

I am a very conceptual person, so I usually imagine these things during the writing and production process, and in the studio, it's a matter of bringing the ideas into life. So on a track like "Anything Can Happen," we listened for cool sounds to accompany the story and set the scene, [such as] jackhammers, honking horns, trains, skidding tires. . . . I think these elements are particularly useful in story songs, because the effects can accent the events being described. We have another song on that same album called "Run for the Light," about a jail-break, and the slamming doors and explosions make the track, in my opinion, much more interesting and fun. But, in the end, we're that kind of group, so it might not work for people who are not so thematic.

Beatboxing

Beatboxing is when drumming with a drum kit is mimicked vocally, by creating the individual drum sounds with your mouth and then performing them in different rhythms. This is a whole skill in itself and can become very complex—it is often done by beatboxers who are not MCs themselves, but who beatbox for MCs to rap over. Occasionally, though, beatboxing is mixed into rapping by an MC or by a beatboxer who also raps.

One of the most notable examples of this is by famed beatboxer Doug E. Fresh on the song "The Show" (03:56), in which he raps alongside Slick Rick and also works in several different beatboxing rhythms and sounds. Similarly, Rahzel sometimes adds parts of his beatboxing into his rap verses. Many MCs who have explored several of the other elements of hip-hop, besides MCing, have been beatboxers at one time or another.

Pigeon John

The first rap group I was in I was the beatboxer . . . [hip-hop] was everywhere, it was coming through the windows when you walked to school, was in the movies with *Krush Groove*, it was just so engulfing, it just kinda took over, when it first started.

El Da Sensei

I was a b-boy and I'd done graffiti, so I always wanted to do everything—I was even doing beatboxing a little bit . . . but I knew that the rhyming part was definitely something I wanted to do [with total focus].

Grunts, Shouts, Laughs, and Other Miscellaneous Sounds

There are many other sounds that are not direct imitations of things but that add extra color and character to a verse.

"Uh," "Huh," "Ahh," "Mmm," "Ha," and "Um"

General grunts such as "uh" and "huh" are used a lot on hip-hop tracks, as they provide an extra syllable or noise to complement the rhythm of the existing lyrics and they blend in well with "real" words. This kind of sound is often improvised while recording.

Andy Cat, Ugly Duckling

Both—[some of those noises are planned, some are improvised]. I love James Brown's music and I really dig the way that he and, especially, Bobby Byrd, pepper the songs with "hehs," "uhs," "ohs," and "heys." For me, it really makes the rhythm swing an extra bit. So, after we've finished the main vocals, I like to go into the booth and record what I call "funk language" and do my best Bobby Byrd impression behind the lyrics and choruses. Hopefully, these little vocal accents will give the songs some extra energy and spontaneity. Q-Tip [of A Tribe Called Quest] is a master of this technique, and that's the reason he's my favorite hip-hop vocalist.

A strong "uh" sound is made by the Lady of Rage on Dr. Dre's song "Lyrical Gangbang" (01:07) ("You think you got pull, then pull it, uh!"), a "huh" is made on Low Profile's "Pay Ya Dues" (03:03) ("Just the other day I turned my radio on, huh!"), an "um" appears on Spice 1's "Trigga Gots No Heart" (01:25) ("Better use that nina, 'cause that deuce-deuce ain't no good, and um . . ."), "ahh" is used on Organized Konfusion's "Stray Bullet" (01:04) ("Ahh, fuck it, next target . . ."), there is a "ha" on the chorus of the Busta Rhymes track "Woo Hah!! Got You All in Check" (00:25), and an "mmm" can be found on Organized Konfusion's "Stray Bullet" (02:30) ("Mmm, Lord, why do they use me?").

"Ooooh" and "Hoooo"

Other popular sounds include "oooohs" and "hoooos." "Oooohs" are often used after a particular hard-hitting line, to imitate how an audience might react with an impressed "ooooh" sound—this happens on the Lady of Rage's "Afro Puffs" (02:42) ("My shit is rude, ooooh"). "Oooohs" can also be used as part of a series of rhythmic sounds, such as on DJ Jazzy Jeff & the Fresh Prince's "Boom! Shake the Room" (01:34) ("Y'all wanna ooooh, ah, ah, ah, ah, ooooh"), and simply for variety in a verse, as on Snoop Dogg's "Serial Killa" (01:32) ("Leave you in a state of paranoia, ooooh").

"Hoooo" is used in a lot of instances to imitate agreement or a chant from a crowd, such as on Dr. Dre's "Keep Their Heads Ringin'" (01:47) ("Three, four for the dough, five for the hoes, hoooo") as well as in the chorus of Naughty by Nature's "Hip-Hop Hooray" (00:18) ("Hip-hop hooraaaay, hoooo").

Big Noyd
[Those crowd type of noises come from] doing things where you got crowd participation, where you sing something and then you make them repeat it, you say something and then

let them finish it, you say half the line and you let them finish the rest.

Other noises are often very similar to these two. Organized Konfusion's "Let's Organize" (02:05) has a "pheeew" noise, Fu-Schnickens's "True Fuschnick" (02:10) includes a "whooo" sound, and Method Man on Wu-Tang Clan's "Protect Ya Neck" (01:47) features a "suuuuuue" sound—all are very similar noises to an "ooooh."

Growls, Yelps, and Clearing the Throat

Growls, yelps, and the sound of clearing your throat also appear on hip-hop tracks. The Pharcyde's "Ya Mama" (03:15) features a growled *r* sound on one of the choruses ("Afffrrrrro with a chiiiiinstrrrrap") and Cypress Hill's "Cock the Hammer" (01:17) also has a growling sound ("Hear me growl, grra-hooowl").

Yelps, which are loud, often higher-pitched bursts of sound, appear on Organized Konfusion's "3-2-1" (00:41) ("One *time* for the mind," where the word "time" is yelped) and on Fu-Schnickens's "Sum Dum Munkey" (01:42) ("Freak it right *now*," where the word "now" is yelped). A throat-clearing sound is heard on Fu-Schnickens's "Hi Lo" (02:44), and the sound is also cleverly worked into a rhythm.

Shock G, Digital Underground

That type of stuff hits artists on the fly. Sometimes I have a loose plan to fill a certain empty space when it comes up, but nothing in particular, just a trust that something good's gonna jump off.

Laughing and Crying

Laughing and crying sounds and deliveries are sometimes used. Laughing sounds occur on LL Cool J's song "Big Ole Butt" (04:08)

and Beastie Boys' "Hey Ladies" (01:02), and are used by 2Pac on
E-40's song "Million Dollar Spot" (01:39). Laughing can also be
worked into the verse as a rhythm, such as on Fu-Schnickens's
tracks "Who Stole the Pebble" (01:24) and "Watch Ya Back" (00:57)
("Heh-heh, hoo-hoo-hoo, ha-haa"), and on Goodie Mob's "Goodie
Bag" (02:58), again worked into a rhythm as part of the verse.

Sometimes laughing is used as a type of delivery, so that other
lyrics are said *while* the MC is laughing, so that they are "laughed"
out—this is done on Fu-Schnickens's "Hi Lo" (02:48). The equivalent of this with a "crying" delivery can be heard on a number of
tracks by Wu-Tang Clan's Ghostface Killah, such as on most of the
Wu-Tang Clan track "I Can't Go to Sleep" (01:00).

Del the Funky Homosapien

You gotta [put yourself] in a different mood to record different types of vocals, definitely. [On the track "I'll Tell You,"
some of the vocals are rapped while laughing.] I can act to a
certain extent, if I have to do it on command. I can conjure
it up and that's basically what it boils down to—if you're a
professional, you're supposed to be able to do whatever it
is that you do on command, otherwise, what's the point of
paying you to do it, if you can't do it when I need you to do it.
So a professional, they work at it to the point where they can
produce whatever they're doing at some level, possibly close
to perfection, during that day.

Various Bodily Sounds

A lot of different bodily sounds are done on records, such as spitting noises, kissing noises, sneezes, hiccups, and snoring. Spitting
noises are done on Das EFX's "Mic Checka" (00:40), Missy Elliot's
"Get Ur Freak On" (01:57), and Spice 1's "Runnin' Out Da Crack-
house" (02:15); kissing noises are done on LL Cool J's "Around the
Way Girl" (02:40), Fu-Schnickens's "Who Stole the Pebble" (01:21),
and A Tribe Called Quest's "Bonita Applebum" (01:59); sneezing

and hiccups appear on Fu-Schnickens's "Breakdown" (01:22 and 01:33); and snoring is heard on Fu-Schnickens's "Sum Dum Munkey" (01:23).

Inhaling, Exhaling, and Out-of-Breath Techniques

Types of breathing can be incorporated as vocal techniques in their own right, such as the noise made when inhaling sharply, as well as breathy sighs and exhales.

Inhaling as Part of Delivery and Rhythm

While most MCs try to inhale silently so that their breaths won't be heard on the recording, a few MCs actually work the loud sound of themselves inhaling into the verse. This adds another sound to the delivery and can become an interesting stylistic element that can be used as part of different rhythms, as if it were another syllable. Method Man of the Wu-Tang Clan noticeably uses this technique in several of his songs, including "Bring the Pain" (02:08) (". . . chest hairs a perm [*inhale*] I don't need a chemical blow to pull a hoe [*inhale*] all I need is . . .") and "Release Yo' Delf" (01:52) ("With my five fingers of death [*inhale*] I bring it to his . . .").

This technique can often come out and become more prominent if you record takes all in one go (as described in the first *How to Rap*, p. 278–280), as you have to make your breaths fit in with the rhythm if you record all in one take.

Killah Priest, Wu-Tang Clan affiliate

As far as being on the mic, sometimes I try to go straight through, straight through the *whole* thing, straight without no punch-ins or nothing. I learned that from Method Man and

RZA, because he always tell me, "Yo, you gonna go straight through it?" It's just a good flow when you go straight through it sometimes. Sometimes you have to go back and edit it.

Exhaling or Sighing

Exhaling or sighing could potentially be used in the same way as inhales, though this is less common. It is usually used to simply add interest with a different noise or to change how a word sounds. Snoop Dogg uses a sigh to begin a verse on his song "Tha Shiznit" (02:23) ("Aaahh, I'm somewhat brain-boggled"), and RBX on Snoop Dogg's "Serial Killa" (02:27) uses an exhale at the end of the word "deep" to alter that word and make it sound distinct ("Deep-aah . . . deep like the minds of Minolta").

Exhaling Through a Syllable

When saying a particular syllable, you can strongly exhale through the word, which gives it a forceful and breathy effect. This is done on Snoop Dogg's "Serial Killa" (01:00 and 02:43), during the lyrics "You can't *come* and you can't *run*" (where "come" and "run" are exhaled on strongly) and "*Bru*tal, jagged, it's totally *rough*neck" (where the syllables "bru" and "rough" are exhaled on). Similarly, on Organized Konfusion's "Stray Bullet" (01:32), the word "hopes" is exhaled through in the phrase "No more dreams, no *hopes* when I spray."

Out of Breath, Wheezing

Delivering a vocal while sounding out of breath or wheezing is also something that can add a lot of character—normally it is seen as a potentially negative thing if an MC doesn't have enough breath to deliver the lyrics, but if it is done in a purposeful way, as a type of style, then it can be very effective.

K-Os

Someone made a comment about it—I did a show in Toronto and I sounded out of breath, and I kinda freaked out a bit. Not an attractive thing live, but when you're in the booth in the studio, and you're in front of a mic with headphones on, you're a lot more aware and delicate about that, I think.

Method Man does this to good effect on the chorus of his track "Release Yo' Delf" (01:45) ("Just *releeeeeeease*" is heavily wheezed), and Ol' Dirty Bastard does it at the end of his verse on Wu-Tang Clan's "Wu-Tang: 7th Chamber" (04:57) ("*Then drop that science*").

Adding a Breath onto the End of a Word

A word can be extended by adding an "ah" type of breath sound to the end of it. This is done on Organized Konfusion's "Black Sunday" (00:01 and 00:27) several times ("help me out-tah," "shirtssah," and "end of the week-kah"), and it helps to keep the delivery interesting.

Beginning a Verse with an Inhale, Then Exhaling the First Sound of the Verse

One way to launch into a verse is to inhale loudly, so that it's heard on the recording, and then strongly exhale while saying the first syllable of the first word of the verse. This is done by the D.O.C. on "Funky Enough" (03:07) ("[*inhale*] I need a break, so I can check around"; the "I" is exhaled strongly at the beginning).

Vocal Trademark Sound or Phrase

MCs sometimes have a vocal trademark—a sound, word, or phrase that is said on a lot of their tracks as a sort of stamp or indication of who is rapping.

For example, Pusha-T of Clipse has used "yeeuk" on several songs, as something to say before or after a particularly hard-hitting line.

Pusha-T, Clipse

[The Neptunes might say,] "Oh, shit, I love that line! After you say that line, why aren't you saying [something to draw attention to how great the line is]? You said something great, [so] tell me something to let me know that you [know the line is great]." Yeeuk—that's where "yeeuk" and all that comes from. You said something great, [so after it, say] "yeeuk."

Other vocal trademarks include MC Eiht's "gyeah," which can be heard right at the beginning of his tracks "Represent" (00:01) and "Thicker Than Water" (00:02), Mystikal's screeching noise of "eeehhhhhn!" at the beginning of tracks like "U Would if You Could" (00:10) and "Danger (Been So Long)" (00:15), Warren G's "whooo!" on his verse from Snoop Dogg's "Ain't No Fun" (03:36) and on his own track "What's Next" (02:12), DMX's dog bark at the beginning of "The Omen" (01:02), and Tech N9ne's "chaa!" throughout his verses on "Caribou Lou" (00:27) and "The Industry Is Punks" (00:50).

Vocal trademarks that may work for one MC may not work for another, so a vocal trademark is usually developed to fit the overall vocal style.

Shock G, Digital Underground

When Too $hort yells, "Biiyeeeooch!" men think it's funny, and women think it's cute. [But] if Xzibit or Rick Ross stands mid-stage and yells that out, it's not cute, it's scary.

Section D | Melodic Deliveries

Mixing Singing and Rapping

As mentioned in the first *How to Rap*, pp. 251–256, rap vocals can be combined with singing to create different types of deliveries. The overall pitch of the MC's voice will often determine the general pitch of the melodies created, as an MC with a low-pitched voice can sing lower notes than an MC with a higher-pitched voice.

Akil the MC, Jurassic 5

Especially with Jurassic 5, [a song] might have melodies in it. If we were doing the chorus and it was something that was melodic for all of us to do together, we would [record] that together and maybe go back and if you needed more [deep] baritone, Chali [2na] could do that or if we needed a [higher melody], Soup could do that.

Shock G, Digital Underground

In the late '70s, a lot of the first hip-hop MCs—Furious Five, Crash Crew, Force MDs—used to have sing routines. We had some of those shows on cassette tapes that circulated at school, and from other Bronx rap legends like Cold Crush Four, Fantastic 5 MCs, Chief Rocker Busy Bee, and even MC Woody-Wood from Brooklyn. Two years before "Rapper's Delight" or "King Tim III" were conceived, they all would bust out the schoolyard-melody, sing-rap routines at the jams and block parties.

Rapping and Singing Sections of a Song

Some MCs like to split a song into different, clearly defined sections—certain parts will be rapped and certain parts will be sung or half-sung. This is a great way to keep the song varied and interesting and to give it a strong, memorable structure.

This happens on Brand Nubian's song "Who Can Get Busy Like This Man" (00:25), which begins with a sung section before the rapped verse comes in. It also happens on Slick Rick's "La Di Da Di" (02:45, although this section is edited out on some versions of the song, due to legal reasons) and on Snoop Dogg's cover of that track, "Lodi Dodi" (02:03), in which the middle section is sung (the section that starts, "It's all because of you, I'm feeling sad and blue"). LL Cool J, on Dr. Dre's "Zoom" (00:27), does his whole first verse in a half-sung delivery, making this a separate section of the song—he then does a more regularly rapped verse later in the song.

Shock G, Digital Underground

I think Queen Latifah was the first blend of a true 100 percent hip-hop MC and a solid musician-capable singer in one person. She had the street cred, the hip-hop authenticity, the lyrical integrity, and the respect of non-hip-hop true singers and musicians of the time. She was the first one of those. Maybe OutKast or Fugees were second and third, and now they're everywhere from the Roots to the Black Eyed Peas. But Queen Latifah was the first one of those that I noticed.

Del the Funky Homosapien

Sometimes singing will keep somebody's attention more— sometimes it might be more appropriate in different parts of the song. It really depends on what the song is asking you to do. Sometimes the song is asking me to sing. I might be walking around the house singing to beats, and I might wanna keep one of those [sections]. That's definitely been a part of [hip-hop] and a lot of times it's the more successful version than just the technical, "I'm killing you, [I'll] chop you down" [type of battle rapping]. Different strokes for different folks, but I feel like if you can bounce back and forth, that's probably the best.

Half-Sung Chanted Sections

Some songs have a section in which the lyrics are half-sung as a sort of chant, which is repeated. This happens at the end of the Pharcyde's "Otha Fish" (03:42), with overlapping, half-sung chants ("You know there's other fish that's in the sea" and "You know there's other, you know that there's other"), and also at the end of their track "Runnin'" (03:59), too ("Can't keep running away, can't keep running away," and "Can't keep running away, running away, running away"). This also features on Bone Thugs-N-Harmony's "Everyday Thang" (02:41) with different chants ("Ooooh, pop in me clip and we come to kill you," "Me killer, me killer," "Come and get me killer, come and get me killer," and "We kill ya").

Bootie Brown, The Pharcyde

At the time [when we started out], we were at this place called SCU, it was like an after-school program, and there was not just MCs there, there was singers and there was producers. It was everything involved in music around us—I think that had a lot to do with it, as far as like singing [and] making choruses for our songs. Instead of every song being the normal hip-hop, three verses and a chorus, we were trying to change it up. I think everybody around us, the singers, the musicians, the producers, the rap artists, and all those types of people being around us, [that] really influenced us as far as us making our music at the time.

Rapping and Singing Within a Verse

Rather than separating the sung and rapped sections of a song, an MC can switch between these two types of delivery within a verse. Snoop Dogg does this a lot, such as on Dr. Dre's "Nuthin' but a G Thang" (00:26) when he half-sings certain words ("Nothing but a G thing, *baaaby*," where the word "baby" is half-sung, while the rest of the line isn't). Mystikal does this on "Danger (Been So Long)" (00:54), half-singing little phrases within the first verse, and Lyrics Born does it on the Latyrx track "Latyrx" (04:37) ("You get your *steeeak and eeeggs*" where "steak and eggs" is half-sung).

Half-Sung Delivery Throughout a Song or Verse

Some MCs who normally rap without a half-sung delivery occasionally adopt a half-sung delivery for a whole verse or song. For example, Lateef of Latyrx, who often raps without a half-sung delivery, uses one for the first verse on Latyrx's "Lady Don't Tek No" (00:20), and the Roots' "DatSkat" is a track that stands out in their catalog for having a half-sung vocal, whereas normally they use a more regular style of rapping.

Shock G, Digital Underground

[There] was the '80s wave of hybrid hip-hop groups and melodic MCs, like Jimmy Spicer, Planet Patrol, Full Force, Jonzun Crew, [Slick Rick, also known as] MC Ricky D's outrageous singing on "La Di Da Di," and especially Queen Latifah, who took rap-singing to a whole 'nother level of believability and harmonic accuracy when she dropped the game-changing "Wrath of My Madness/Princess of the Posse" single in '88.

Del the Funky Homosapien

I know Slick Rick used to do that and I was a huge Slick Rick fan, so I would have to assume that, yeah, I got it from him, but I also used to listen to regular songs before hip-hop came out, so I guess it's part of that too. I guess some of it has to do with teasing like, "nah na-nah, na-nah nah," some of it comes from that. Nursery rhymes . . . think about all the [things] you heard in your life that could be an influence, like Dr. Seuss. I'm sure stuff from your childhood probably inadvertently or inexplicably just hops in the mix too, from your subconscious.

Half-Sung Delivery as Part of the Overall Vocal Style

There are MCs who use a half-sung delivery on almost all of their songs as an inherent part of their vocal style, which makes them recognizable and separates them from most other MCs. These range from deliveries that are very close to regular singing, such as by SlimKid Tre of the Pharcyde, Domino, and Bone Thugs-N-Harmony; to MCs who often half-sing lyrics, such as Slick Rick, Lyrics Born, Nelly, and Speech of Arrested Development; to MCs who have very melodic voices, so that even though they may not actually be half-singing during songs, their voices always have a melodic quality to them, such as Snoop Dogg, Warren G, Devin the Dude, and Schoolly D.

Nelly

I think [the half-sung delivery], that's one of the distinctive things I've been able to do, I think it's just come over a period of time of the music that you do. I grew up on a lot of different groups, hip-hop was in when I was growing up, but it wasn't the predominant music like it is now. It was still more of the R&B and the soul type of feel, a lot of melodies, a lot of feeling, so I kind of combined it, [rapping and singing together].

Singing Part of Another Song

A popular way of incorporating singing into a hip-hop verse is by singing part of another song that has sung lyrics—either using the original lyrics or altering them in some way. Of course, the more musical knowledge you have, in all genres, the more songs and melodies you can draw from and interpolate in your own lyrics and make reference to.

Myka 9, Freestyle Fellowship

I mainly learned [about music and rapping] by repeating songs that I would hear on the radio or repeating songs that I would hear my parents play. They played Blowfly, they played "King Tim III," [by the] Fatback [Band], they had some Teena Marie records, they had some Deborah Harry records, back in the Blondie days, some of the jazz records they had too, they had more of a rhythmic sort of delivery, even the old Dolomite records. I would sneak in and listen to the Blowfly records, I think Blowfly was one of the first rappers. I think my pops had a Last Poets record, too.

As a Separate Section

Slick Rick on "La Di Da Di" (02:45, although this section is edited out on some versions of the song, due to legal reasons) sings part of the melody of A Taste of Honey's song "Sukiyaki" ("It's all because of you, I'm feeling sad and blue") and also part of Dionne Warwick's "Walk on By" on "Mona Lisa" (02:41). In both these cases, the re-sung parts are placed into their own sections, rather than being placed in the middle of a verse.

Stressmatic, The Federation

[On the track "I Wear My Stunna Glasses at Night,"] Rick Rock had come up with the concept, he was like, "Y'all should redo that Corey Hart song ['I Wear My Sunglasses at Night']." He sent me the old Corey Hart song, so I was just in my bedroom playing it over and over and then I just wrote the chorus. Then I shot it to Marty James, who sang the hook—he sang it and we all went into the studio and recorded it.

Del the Funky Homosapien

Slick Rick was definitely somebody that did that—sing other people's lyrics as a reference in his music: "Michelle, ma belle," [on "The Show," referencing the Beatles' "Michelle"]. He might do that to reference another song, just to be clowning in the song he's doing.

As Part of a Rapped Verse

On the Fugees' track "Cowboys" (02:50), part of Kenny Rogers's "The Gambler" is resung ("Got to know when to hold them, know when to fold them"). This is done in the middle of a verse, rather than made into its own separate section of the song. Similarly, on Big Daddy Kane's "Show and Prove" (02:53) he sings part of Isaac Hayes's "Theme from Shaft" ("Now tell me, who is the man?") during the beginning of his verse—he also works in the lyrics of the re-sung song into his own verse by doing this (extending the "Who is the man?" lyrics from "Theme from Shaft" with his own lyrics: ". . . with the high-potent lyrics, no rapper can ever stand").

Altering the Lyrics

Although sometimes the exact lyrics from the original song are resung, often the lyrics are altered in some way to fit the rapped lyrics and for humorous effect. This is done on Fu-Schnickens's "True Fuschnick" (01:29) when part of Manfred Mann's song "Do Wah Diddy Diddy" is resung with altered lyrics ("Doo-wah, diddy, diddy, dum, diddy Fu," where "Fu" replaces the final syllable, which is "doo" in the original song).

Devin the Dude

[The humor in my songs] comes from just back in the day before there was hip-hop and stuff, I used to always listen to comedy albums. I used to listen to comedy albums like I did

R&B records, and when I finally got a chance to get inside the booth and do music, I kind of incorporated the humor in the hip-hop and the hard beats and stuff together.

Rapping a Sung Melody

Usually, the song being used in a rap verse is resung close to the original melody and rhythm, though occasionally the same lyrics are used, but rapped instead of sung, sometimes in a different rhythm. This is done by Method Man on the Wu-Tang Clan song "Method Man" (01:30) when he raps lyrics from the Rolling Stones' "Get Off of My Cloud" ("Hey, you, get off my cloud, you don't know me and you don't know my style").

Half-Sung Delivery Techniques

Although singing is an entire area of study in its own right, separate from rapping, there are some general techniques that are used when MCs half-sing certain rap lyrics. In the first *How to Rap*, techniques such as matching the melody of another instrument in the music as well as creating a different melody to complement the existing melodies (*How to Rap*, p. 252) were mentioned. Here are some further techniques.

Higher-Pitched Line Followed by Lower-Pitched Line

A very common melodic technique is to raise the pitch for a line, then "resolve" the melody by going down in pitch on the next line. In half-sung rapping, a raised pitch mimics the sound of someone asking a question, while a lowered pitch sounds more like someone making a statement—so if a melody ends with a raised pitch, it makes it feel like the melody has been left "unanswered," left hanging, while ending with a lower pitch feels more like the melody has been "answered" or "resolved."

Because of this, you often get a first line that has a raised pitch to "ask the question" with the melody, and then a second line with a lowered pitch to "answer the question" with the melody. (Often, there is no actual question being asked and answered in the content of the lyrics. This asking and answering is purely the feeling that is created by raising and lowering the pitch.)

This resolution of the melody is used in other genres of music and with other instruments (when an "unstable"-sounding note is followed by a more "stable"- or "final"-sounding one, to "resolve" it), but it is particularly noticeable in half-sung rapping, because it is so close to actual speech, in which raising pitch is used for questions and a lowered pitch is used for statements.

Of course, this technique is not compulsory—there are no "rules"—but it is used a lot. It is satisfying to listen to, because the "question" is resolved at the end.

An example of this is on Snoop Dogg's "G Funk Intro" (01:25), with the following lyrics:

> This is just a small introduction to the G Funk era, [*up in pitch*]
> Every day of my life I take a glimpse in the mirror [*back down to regular pitch*]
> And I see motherfuckers trying to be like me [*up in pitch*]
> Ever since I put it down with the D, R, E . . . [*down in pitch*]

As we can see, the first phrase is raised in pitch, while the second goes back down to a more regular-voiced pitch. The third line then raises the pitch again, and the final line goes back down, particularly on the final "E," which goes a lot further down in pitch to resolve the entire melody and to signal the end of the half-sung section.

Another example is on the Pharcyde's "Runnin'" (01:52):

There comes a time in every man's life [*up in pitch*]
When he's gotta handle shit, upon his own, [*down in pitch*]
Can't depend on friends to help you in a squeeze, [*up in pitch*]
Please, they got problems of their own. [*down in pitch*]

The end of the first phrase is raised, while the end of the second
falls in pitch. The same pattern happens again with the third and
fourth lines—the third line goes up in pitch, and then is answered
by the fourth line's drop in pitch.

This technique is often used to better complement the beat—
often the level of complexity of the rhythms and rhymes may be
sacrificed in order to fit more melodically with the track that is
being rapped over. MCs who also make beats are often concerned
with how the vocal will enhance the beat, rather than just trying to
rap as impressively as possible.

Thes One, People Under the Stairs

Being a beat-maker first meant that instead of sitting around
writing rhymes and thinking about how awesome our rhymes
were, we were busy studying old records and reading biogra-
phies of old musicians and really kinda getting rooted in the
bigger picture of music. And so by the time it came around
to actually writing, we were looking at it differently, we were
looking at it like, "How can we put something over these beats
to make them better?" I think in terms of hip-hop, I tend to
appreciate people who complement a beat more than people
who come out and [just rap] really, really [well].

Out of Tune

Although MCs generally want to be in tune so that the melodies
of their voices are not clashing with the melodies of the music
they're rapping over, being out of tune can sometimes be used to

surprise the listener or for humorous effect, or simply as part of an overall style.

Ol' Dirty Bastard did a number of songs with out-of-tune singing, such as on his verse on the remix to Mariah Carey's "Fantasy" (03:04) and on Wu-Tang Clan's song "Dog Shit" (00:11). This worked very well for Ol' Dirty Bastard, as it fit in with his overall wild and untamed style as an artist and his vocal delivery. Similarly, Biz Markie sings out of tune on "Just a Friend" (00:58), which complements his humorous, playful style and gives his tracks a lot of personality.

It may even help to have less knowledge about melody in order to pull off out-of-tune singing, as knowing how to sing in tune makes it harder to purposely sing out of tune.

Shock G, Digital Underground

[Knowing music theory] can go from blessing to curse when I wanna *not* make so much music sense, like say Kanye's singing. Sometimes he gives it just the right amount of off-key-ness.

Changing Voice for Melodies

Some MCs half-sing with a voice that is very much like their regular rapping voice, while others adopt a different style for the half-sung elements. For example, Big Daddy Kane on "Show and Prove" (02:53) imitates Isaac Hayes's vocal style when he resings some of the lyrics from Isaac Hayes's song "Theme from Shaft," rather than singing it in his own regular vocal style.

Matching Patterns and Half-Sung Deliveries

Lots of half-sung deliveries work well with rhythms that have "matching patterns" as described in the first *How to Rap*, p. 119

(patterns created by using the same rhythm on several bars so that the bars "match"). This is done on Snoop Dogg's "Gin and Juice" (00:33) when he half-sings the following lyrics:

1	2	3	4
May	I	**kick** a little	**some**thing for the
Gs	and	**make** a few	**ends** as I
breeze	through	**two** in the	**morn**ing and the . . .

Put into a pattern diagram (from the first *How to Rap*, p. 116), which shows how many syllables are in each quarter of the bar, we can see that the rhythm closely matches from bar to bar:

1st	2nd	3rd	4th
1	1	4	4
1	1	3	3
1	1	3	4

As can be seen, the 1st and 2nd quarters of each bar have one syllable in them, while the 3rd and 4th quarters all have either three or four syllables—so each bar has a similar rhythmic pattern. This is common in half-sung deliveries, as it reinforces the melody if the rhythm repeats from bar to bar in this way.

Mighty Casey

You might wanna make sure you're doing all 16 [bars] in the same flow pattern just to keep a consistent, catchy flow [if you're doing a party song].

Rah Digga

I'm not even mad at the [more] simple, sing-along stuff—the rest of the album [or song] can be super-intricate with the lyrics and everything, but in order to get that initial reaction, to get the heads turning, you [sometimes] gotta hit them with the catchy stuff first.

Pharoahe Monch

I think that was the beauty of hip-hop back then [when it first started]—a lot of the simpler songs are easy to remember and those are the songs that get you hooked at first.

Section E | Character, Personality, and Emotions

Character and Personality

With many of the best MCs' vocals, their voices give you a lot of information about their character before you even begin to pay attention to *what* they're saying—you don't have to know what type of music they do or have heard any of their content, as their delivery gives you a lot to go on from the start.

This is often something that affects the listener even if he or she can't quite tell why. This is why you can hear a really technically good MC, with perfect rhythm and rhyme schemes, but still be bored, if there is no life, character, or distinct quality to his or her voice. Most MCs begin by taking some of the characteristics of other MCs they like, and later refining their own character and really pinning down their own vocal style.

R.A. the Rugged Man

When I first started rhyming, we was trying to rap like our idols, that's when you're [like], "OK, I'm gonna rap like Rakim this month." And then when [Grand] Puba came out and was really blowing up and Brand Nubian was crazy, you're sitting there [trying to sound like Grand Puba], like trying to be all bouncy on some Puba shit. You ain't discovered your own style yet, so you've gotta find yourself.

The techniques we've looked at so far are all responsible for adding character and personality to the vocal delivery, though certain combinations of these techniques are what gives a particular overall effect to the vocal and makes the delivery style distinct. The following are some general personality types and how these often come through in the delivery.

Energetic, Wild, Unpredictable, and Humorous

MCs who are energetic and unpredictable with a strong sense of humor often have this quality in their voices, too. MCs such as Busta Rhymes, Ol' Dirty Bastard, and Flavor Flav of Public Enemy all have deliveries that express this kind of personality—they tend to vary the volume, timbre, and pitch of their voices a lot, while including lots of additional noises, sound effects, out-of-tune singing, and other techniques to keep the vocal unpredictable and unrestrained.

Termanology

Back in the days [there was a lot of innovation], because everybody had their own style. You could come out screaming, you could come out like Busta Rhymes if you wanted to, you could come out like however.

Fun, Playful, and Bouncy

Some MCs are very playful and bouncy and enjoy themselves a lot on a track, such as Eminem (in his Slim Shady alter ego), the Pharcyde, Souls of Mischief, and B-Real of Cypress Hill. There is a lot of playful use of pitch, and higher-pitched voices tend to be used. Sound effects and character voices are often created or imitated as well.

B-Real, Cypress Hill

["Insane in the Brain"] . . . it's a bouncy type of song. We didn't think it was a hit when we first did it, [but] we knew it was a good song and once we played it live people were going to go crazy, [because it's bouncy].

Serious and Authoritative

KRS-One, Chuck D, Big Daddy Kane, and Melle Mel are all generally serious and authoritative on records, and this comes through in their voices as they use louder volume levels; clear, deep timbres; and rising and falling pitch to create strong statements and questions.

Calm, Cool, and Laid-Back

MCs such as Snoop Dogg, Devin the Dude, Slick Rick, and Shock G of Digital Underground all have relaxed, chilled personalities, and again this comes through strongly just from their voices. They tend to rap at a regular-voice volume, with a smooth timbre, adding a lot of relaxed, half-sung melodies. They all give a very laid-back vibe to the track through the sound of their voices.

Speech, Arrested Development

Another example [of a great personality] would be Snoop, who as just a general character in hip-hop, I enjoy hearing him flow.

Introspective and Poetic

MCs such as 2Pac, Nas, Kool G Rap, Rakim, and O.C. of Diggin' in the Crates are examples of artists who have deep, introspective personalities. Their voices reflect this by being restrained in terms of volume and timbre, but with the ability to express emotion in the right places, through a controlled use of pitch.

Angry and Annoyed

Ice Cube and Mystikal are MCs who often sound angry and harsh on records, which is good for politically themed songs as well as making sarcastic, cutting punch lines. Using a loud volume with a harsh timbre, as well as raising pitch on certain words and phrases, can create this effect and this type of character.

Esoteric

If I'm spitting something aggressive, it probably sounds closer to when I'm at the Registry of Motor Vehicles trying to get my business straight—a voice closer to a yell. If the beat is driven by sinister violins and shrill piano stabs, you want to match the hardcore feel of the track, thus raising your voice and attitude.

Having Fun with Vocals to Bring Out Your Personality

A lot of the best vocal takes have an element of casualness and fun to them, as an MC's actual personality comes through more easily if he or she is having a good time and fully expressing his or her character. If a vocal take is too carefully crafted, it can lose the energy and appeal that it would have with a bit more looseness.

MCs and groups who put a lot of energy and fun into the delivery and aren't afraid to "color outside of the lines" include the Pharcyde, Busta Rhymes, Fu-Schnickens, Das EFX, Ol' Dirty Bastard, Snoop Dogg, Shock G of Digital Underground, Method

Man, and a lot of others who are known for their strong personalities on records.

Imani, The Pharcyde

I have fun making music, so part of the fun is the process of making it—I don't like trying to be [overly] precise all the time, I like to have some fun. I mean, I'm not saying that you can't have fun and be precise, but I'm just saying for me, [the fun is part of] the creative process.

The character and personality come through in the fun and enjoyment you can hear in someone's voice—listeners can easily pick up on this element.

Pigeon John

That's why I love hip-hop—when you hear the Pharcyde or something like that, you can tell that they were not trying to get anything across as far as anything but a good time.

Wordsworth

I learned how to rap just really practicing freestyling outside, just from having fun outside, man. If you ain't having fun doing it, for the most part you're not going to rap. It doesn't matter if you're doing it for money or whatever the case, whatever you doing it for, there has to be some type of enjoying it for the fun of it.

Emotions

Some MCs are masters at expressing their emotions through their voices, so even if they are speaking in another language, you would still be able to tell whether they are sad, angry, happy, joking, and so on, because it comes through very strongly in their voices.

Listeners respond to this—it's easier to feel an emotional connection to an MC if you can tell he or she is feeling that emotion, because you're hearing it in his or her voice. You can rap about being really, really angry, but if you're doing it in a soft, gentle voice, it won't register as much with the listener, because they won't be able to "hear" your anger.

Del the Funky Homosapien

My vocal range is pretty good, I can play with it, come across with different emotion. I'm a Leo. . . . Leos are natural actors.

Pusha-T, Clipse

Hell Hath No Fury, a lot of that album was just a bitter place and time, a terrible, bitter, disgusting place in time, so if it sounded super demonic or angry or whatever, it was. I think a lot of people can hear that, too.

Capturing Emotions on Record

As with character and personality, emotions can be expressed by using the techniques already covered, such as changes in pitch, volume, and timbre, and by additional techniques such as vibrato and melody.

Although you can plan which techniques to use, it can also be useful to actually get into the emotion and really feel it, by recalling something that makes you feel the actual emotion, whether it's anger, happiness, sadness, or another emotion. The music you're rapping over might itself evoke the emotion in you.

Yukmouth

If it's a slow type of sad song, I'll make some sad shit, some reminiscing, storytelling shit, and make the hook real sad, so I go with the music. Whatever the direction the music is going in, that's where I'm going.

B-Real, Cypress Hill

Sometimes I just let the music take me wherever I think the music is going, whether it's a dark, moody vibe or something humorous, or something that's a good-time, party type of atmosphere.

Sometimes an MC will record a take and the emotion will be perfect, but the words are slightly out of time or there is a small mistake. This is sometimes fixed in the studio with studio software by punching-in (described in the first *How to Rap*, p. 274), because the MC might not be able to convey the emotion as well in another take.

Evidence, Dilated Peoples

If I like a take I did and [I'm like], "Damn, the emotion was there but the pocket wasn't," then I'll just go in and move one part a little bit here and keep the take, because I like the way I did it. It's more about emotion than it is anything else.

With a very emotional song, such as the Pharcyde's "Passin' Me By," it can be very important to get the emotion coming through the voice and delivery correctly—so much so that one take may be significantly better than another.

Bootie Brown, The Pharcyde

"Passin' Me By," my verse actually came off a cassette tape that I did in a studio. I didn't go to the big studio and then rerecord and it was all great, I went to the big studio and tried to rerecord and people were like, "Nah, that's not the same, it doesn't sound the same!" And I was like, man, I don't know, I don't know, and they were like, "Man, we're just going to use the one off the cassette—that sounds best," and that's the one that I used.

Some MCs like to record vocals as they write them, so as they are feeling the emotion from the writing process, they can immediately go and record that emotion, through their voice.

David Banner

If I write a whole song [down], I end up losing the [vocal] style. So, especially with [today's music production software], I'll write a line and spit that line, because I'm emotional about that line or that half a verse, then I'll go write some more. So then that makes every verse and every line powerful—there's no throwaway lines [that way].

Expressing a Range of Emotions

Two of the most popular MCs, 2Pac and Eminem, are noted for their ability to translate their emotions clearly onto records. Listeners often connect very strongly with this, as it lets them know the MC is going through the same emotions that they are and that they're not rapping just in a technically impressive way.

Examples of 2Pac's vocal deliveries with a lot of clear emotion to them are: "Hit 'Em Up" (anger), "I Get Around" (happiness), "Life Goes On" (sadness), "Only God Can Judge Me" (pain), "Keep Ya Head Up" (hope), "Dear Mama" (love), "How Do You Want It" (lust), and "Only Fear of Death" (fear/paranoia). Eminem songs with the same kind of strong emotion coming through the vocal takes are "Kim" (anger), "The Way I Am" (frustration), "The Real Slim Shady" (happiness), "Mockingbird" (sadness), and "Lose Yourself" (determination).

The music used to rap over is often responsible for bringing out a wide range of emotions—this is why picking the right beats is an important skill for any MC.

Andy Cat, Ugly Duckling

That's what makes the legends [like] Rakim, KRS-One, Big Daddy Kane, Kool G Rap, Q-Tip, [and Grand] Puba [of Brand Nubian] legendary—their ability to capture a wide range of emotion and attitude. And one of the secrets is that in the "classic" era, the music was intricately produced and arranged, sounding close to funk, jazz, and soul music. It's best to have dynamic and interesting music if you are going to use these techniques.

Sometimes it can be interesting to express an emotion in the vocal delivery that isn't the same sentiment that is expressed in the actual content of the song—in a way, "hiding" the content by giving a different impression through the delivery.

Pigeon John

I think that's kinda cool, [when] the song can sound happy and you can be talking about [something a lot more serious], and you have [kids] singing along and the soccer moms and they have no idea. I think it's more sneaky that way, versus giving an intro like, "Yo, this song is about all the mothers trying to work hard, trying to feed their babies" [and making it obvious you're being serious in your voice].

3

Advanced Rhyme Techniques

Study the blueprints, man, the blueprints is there. The advice
I would give is go back and listen to us, listen to [Kool] G Rap,
[Big Daddy] Kane, Rakim, Slick Rick, Public Enemy, KRS[-One],
Redman, Wu[-Tang Clan] . . .
◄ O.C., Diggin' in the Crates ►

The first *How to Rap* described a number of different rhyme techniques and rhyme schemes. However, many variations and extra
techniques are also used. The following part of this book looks at
some of the most effective additional approaches that MCs use.
The emphasis here is on techniques that can be heard relatively
clearly and that make a real tangible difference to the flow, rather
than complexity that looks good on paper but that listeners are
unable to pick up on.

Also, be aware that advanced rhyming is not a new phenom-
enon and that simply rhyming at a high level will not make you
stand out from the crowd—it has to be an element of a larger,
more distinct style.

R.A. the Rugged Man
Do your own shit, [but also] study what everyone around you
is doing and know what's around you. And learn your history

of the music, too, because what happens is if you don't know your history you might do some shit you think you just originated, and think you're fly, [but you're] doing some shit that somcone did 15 years ago.

Runs of Rhyme

A technique that is used by many of the most acclaimed lyricists is doing a section of a song in which many rhymes are packed into each bar of music. This is done by combining two techniques described in the first *How to Rap*: "Compound Rhymes" (p. 87) and "Number of Rhymes in a Bar" (p. 104).

This is a popular technique, because it sounds immediately impressive. Rather than rhymes spread out in a verse, the rhymes are all tightly packed together one after the other, and so can be heard easily by the listener. The music being rapped over can also be a reason for choosing this type of rhyming, and conversely, this type of rhyming may also influence how an MC chooses beats.

Esoteric

My personal preference is to include a lot of multisyllabic rhymes. It may give you the impression that I pick beats based on drums, but I think the mood set by basslines or pianos have a lot to do with it, too.

The following is a breakdown of how different lengths of compound rhyme look and sound within this technique.

One-Syllable Rhymes

One way of doing a run of rhymes is with single-syllable rhymes, in which the same one-syllable sound is repeated over and over.

This means many syllables can all be made to rhyme within a bar, because potentially the whole bar could be full of syllables, all with the same sound.

Big Daddy Kane's "Wrath of Kane" (01:33) has a good example of one-syllable rhymes repeated often throughout a couplet:

1	2	3	4
I come to **teach** and	**preach** and reach	**and** each.	
With the **speech** every	**leech** I'll im-	**peach**.	

Runs of one syllable rhymes were used a lot in the late 1980s, as MCs were pushing the artform forward and adding more and more rhymes. As longer compound rhymes became more popular during the early 1990s, one-syllable rhymes became less common, though it is still an impressive technique, especially as a variation on longer compound rhymes.

R.A. the Rugged Man

Early '80s they were changing up the flow, late '80s with [Big Daddy] Kane, he started doing a lot of that changing the flow shit.

Two-Syllable Compound Rhymes

Runs of two-syllable-long compound rhymes are possibly the most common form of packing more rhymes into each bar. They have more variation in their sound than one-syllable rhymes, because they contain two sounds instead of one and they can still fit a lot of rhymes in per bar (unlike longer compound rhymes, which we will look at later).

Here is an example from Blackalicious's "Deep in the Jungle" (01:25):

1	2	3	4
Gifted when I'm	**lift**ed off a spliff	**hit**, reminisce shit,	**riff** with dipshits.
This shit is a	**mis**fit style of the	**gift**ed. I'm a whiz	**kid**, get a whiff, kid …

In these two bars there are 11 compound rhymes, which are all two syllables in length, giving it a very fast and impressive feel as the rhymes run on from one another. The compound rhymes are "gifted," "lifted," "spliff hit," "-isce shit," "riff with," "dipshits," "this shit," "misfit," "gifted," "whiz kid," and "whiff, kid."

Gift of Gab, Blackalicious

[On] "Deep in the Jungle," me and Lateef and Lyrics just sat down and vibed out and we were talking about we want to make it ill, we want to make it stylistic, we want to make it different, we don't want it to sound like anything that's out there, we want it to be completely its own thing. I hadn't heard nobody rap like that before that. And I did it and I left it alone, I didn't have to stay with it—I'm a traveler, I'ma create more styles.

Brother J, X Clan

When [Big Daddy] Kane came out, everybody was, "*Going* and *showing* and *flowing*" and so on, and doing all that [continuous rhyming].

Three-Syllable Compound Rhymes

Three-syllable compound rhymes can be used to create a run of rhymes as well. Not as many of them can be packed into a bar as one- and two-syllable rhymes, but longer phrases can be created, giving more scope to create more complicated rhymes.

This example from Kool G Rap's verse on Sway and King Tech's "The Anthem" (02:42) demonstrates a run of three-syllable compound rhymes (which continues throughout the entire verse):

1	2	3	4
Tech with the	**Tech** and Sway	**step** away,	**wet** and spray,
rep the day who	**over** debt to	**pay** get swept a-	**way** and cross the . . .

The compound rhymes "Tech and Sway," "step away," "wet and spray," and "rep the day" all fall directly on the beat in the first bar and at the start of the second, though it finishes with two compound rhymes that fall across beats, "debt to pay," and "swept away," which add more variation.

Hell Rell, Dipset

I try to make at least every last three words rhyme with each other.

This degree of rhyming is often easier to do with more open-ended content, because if the song has a very specific message or concept, it may be harder to clearly present the message within the run of rhymes.

Shock G, Digital Underground

Usually you have to make a decision before you begin: "Shall I favor meaning and content, or flow?" If you choose to make every word of every sentence rhyme perfectly with every word of every other sentence, the message [might not] be stated at optimum impact, and vice versa. I believe it's easier to keep a perfect and consistent pattern going when sticking to the easy topics—how dope me, my clique, my neighborhood is, [and] how wack you and yours are. But if you're trying to tackle a specific issue, and trying to maintain passion, emotional impact, clarity of position, and factual accuracy, [then you might] need to sacrifice some flow.

Tech N9ne

It's hard to rhyme and make sense at the same time [sometimes], especially when you do what I do—you want to make it exciting. So if I'm talking about something like [in the lyrics of "This Ring" (01:03)]: "This ring, got me a top-notch, straight hot fox, we sought rocks . . . dropped two, playing hopscotch on the block," it sounds like just a lot of rhyming words, people love it, but if you listen to it, I'm talking about how I met my wife. "Got me a top-notch, straight hot fox, we sought rocks," [means] we went out and bought rings, "Dropped two, playing hopscotch on the block" [means] we had two little girls. To make sense and still make it fun for the MC or the people to listen to, it's a hard thing to do.

Longer Compound Rhymes

With some longer compound rhymes, it may not be possible to fit many of them within each bar, as there may only be room for one or two.

For instance, on Slick Rick's "I Own America" (00:08), he uses six-syllable compound rhymes:

1	2	3	4
	All of you	**cock**-pullers are	**front**ing,
wave your arms a-	**round** like you're an	**oct**opus or	**some**thing . . .

The compound rhymes are "cock pullers are fronting" rhyming with "octopus or something." As they both take up half a bar, it would not be possible to repeat the compound rhymes many times, as there is only so much space in each bar.

The same thing happens in Eminem's "Lose Yourself" (01:18) with six-syllable compound rhymes:

1	2	3	4
Oh, there goes	**Rabbit** he	**choked**. He's so	**mad** but he
won't give up	**that** easy.	**No**, he won't	**have** it, he . . .

The compound rhymes of, "oh there goes Rabbit he," "choked he's so mad but he," "won't give up that easy," and "no he won't have it he," take up half a bar each, and so only two will fit into each bar (they rhyme through the use of the "linking with rhythm" type of compound rhyme, explained in the first *How to Rap*, p. 90).

This is a popular way of adding a lot of complexity to the verse, but bear in mind that it can be good to explore other styles of rhyming, rather than only focusing on increasing the complexity of the compound rhymes.

Esoteric

I thought rhyming three- or four-syllable words was enough, like in my mind nobody was coming up with the words I was coming up with, nobody was rhyming this word with that word, like that's my shit. Like, I'm gonna aim for like a four-syllable rhyme right now, just really compounding the shit. And that was like my angle, that's why I thought I was nice and then I realized I have to start delivering the rhymes different, switching my flow a little bit.

Alliteration and Consonance Runs of Rhyme

Another way to create a run of similar sounds is to use alliteration or consonance, rather than using perfect rhyme, assonance, or bending words. As explained in *How to Rap* (pp. 86–87), alliteration occurs when words begin with the same letter or sound and consonance is created when the consonant sounds in a word are the same but the vowel sound is different.

Here is an example from Pharoahe Monch's "Hell" (00:28):

1	2	3	4
Focus upon the	fact that	facts can be	fabricated to
form lies.		My phonetics a-	lone forces . . .

The "f" consonant sound is repeated continuously, as a run of alliteration, with the words "focus," "fact," "facts," "fabricated," "form," "phonetics," and "forces."

Planet Asia

[Some people just rhyme] on the 4, where you ain't really caring about the in between, like "when I come to the party . . . I see everybody," like you're not even doing nothing in between, just leaving a space. [But] you could be like "musical, majesty, masterful. . . ." It can go any kind of way you want it to go.

Alternate Rhyme Scheme Patterns

The vast majority of rhyme schemes in rapping involve rhyming words that link together bars that are next to each other. For example, couplets link two bars next to each other, and a multiliner rhyme scheme (*How to Rap*, p. 101) over six bars would link together six bars in a row, without skipping any bars.

However, there are some rhyme schemes that aren't used as frequently, in which a longer, more drawn-out pattern will emerge. This is generally not done as much because it has a different effect—if a rhyme on the first bar of a verse then only rhymes with something on the fourth bar, for example, then the rhyming effect isn't as immediate, because there is a bigger gap between the rhymes. Whereas when rhyme schemes use rhymes in quick succession, the rhymes can be heard more easily.

An example of a more drawn out rhyme scheme is on Cypress Hill's "Pigs" (00:25):

1	2	3	4
This pig ha-	**rassed** the whole	**neighbor-**	**hood**, well
this pig	**worked** at the	**sta-**	**tion**,
This pig	**he** killed my	**home**boy	**so** the fucking
pig	**went** on a va-	**cation**.	

Here, the rhyme scheme rhymes "station" on the second bar, with "-cation" on the fourth bar. This means that the first and third bars do not have rhymes on them—normally these bars would have some kind of connecting rhymes, too. This pattern is used throughout the song and gives it a distinct feel, as it differs from most other rap rhyme schemes. Another rare instance of this kind of pattern is at the beginning of the second verse of the Pharcyde's "Runnin'."

An example of a pattern that is also more spread out, but in a different sequence, is on A Tribe Called Quest's "If the Papes Come" (01:00):

1	2	3	4
Letter to the	**home**boy that	**freaked** the head	**dome**, the
army wants	**me** to	**drop** my micro-	**phone**.
Gotta be	*brief,* no	**ord**ers from a	*chief,* hot
butter on	**what**, say	**what**, the pop-	**corn**

Here, the main rhyme is on the first and second bars, then it skips a bar and the third bar has its own single-line rhyme scheme of "brief" and "chief," and then the main rhyme returns as the line ends with "corn," which is said in such a way that it rhymes with "dome" and "phone." This pattern repeats for every four bars of the song. A similar rhyme scheme is also used on Dizzee Rascal's song "Fix Up, Look Sharp."

Using this type of pattern often makes the song sound closer to a "regular" song from genres outside of hip-hop, in which rhymes are usually not so tightly packed together.

Brother Ali

I approach rapping like being a musician—I approach it like I'm singing. Me and Ant, and I would include Slug [of the group Atmosphere] in this, too, we all approach it like we're making songs. We're not making raps, we're making music. So we want to do it the same way that a blues musician or a rock musician [does it], or jazz or reggae or whatever. Ant comes into this as a DJ [and] as a hip-hop producer, and we come into it as MCs, but we're trying to use what we have to make music, [rather than just specifically hip-hop], and so my cadence and my flow and my delivery is coming from that kind of place.

Pigeon John

I look at a lot of different other formats of songs that don't necessarily have a [hip-hop] pattern of rhyme and it's more of poems and stuff, like Jim Morrison or whatever, [where] they were poems before they became songs.

An even longer pattern in a similar style appears on Blackalicious's "Swan Lake" (01:06). The rhyming words are shown here, with the rest of the lyrics replaced with dashes, to make it easier to see the pattern:

1	2	3	4
-------- --	--- -- ---	--- --------- ---	**tide** ---
---- -- ----- ---	------- -	---- ---- ---- -	**ride** -- ---
----- --- --	------- -- ---	---- ----	**sides** -- ----
------- -----	-- --- -	<u>par</u>ty	---
-------- -----	---- --- --	---- -----	*heads* - --- ---
----- ---- --	----- -- --- ----	------- --	*shreds* -- -----
------- ---- ---	---- -------	--- ---	*Keds* -----
- ----	--- ------- --	--	<u>body</u>

The first part of the pattern is a rhyme scheme that begins with "tide," "ride," and "sides" linking the first three bars together. Then on the fourth bar, the word "party" appears, seemingly un-rhymed at this point. Then a new rhyme scheme begins, joining another three bars, with "heads," "shreds," and "Keds." The final bar of the eight-bar pattern then ends with word "body"—this rhymes with the word "party" from the fourth bar, creating a rhyme scheme that links the fourth and eighth bars in this pattern. The same pattern is used throughout the song, giving it a very clear and memorable structure.

These "simpler" types of rhyme scheme, with fewer rhyming words spread out over more bars of music, may not have the complexity of other patterns, but not every track and beat calls for maximum complexity.

Thes One, People Under the Stairs

[Writing our lyrics doesn't take that] long, because we're not really "super scientifical." I mean, we could sit down and write the "super-scientifical, super-lyrical-miracle" [style of rhymes with everything rhyming], but it's just not what we're trying to do and it's not what we like listening to. So I'm not trying to do a [style] where I'm cramming 4,000 words into two bars and at the same time I'm not doing [a really basic style], but I'd say I'm closer to the [simpler style] than I am to the [complex style].

Zumbi, Zion I

[Previously,] I would try to impress the listener with how verbose I could be, how many words I could put in this little space. [But] nowadays it's more about the feeling, the phrasing and making it just feel very organic, but then still say something that will catch the listener's attention. It's just a more simple approach now, I think, than before.

Joining Rhyme Schemes Together

There are several ways to join rhymes together or to make them interact in some way. This can add another level of complexity to the rhyme schemes and create more variety as well.

Morphing One Rhyme Scheme into the Next

One rhyme scheme can be morphed into another one by retaining some of the rhyming words from one scheme to be used in the next scheme.

This is done on Nas's "N.Y. State of Mind" (00:22):

1	2	3	4
Rappers, I	monkey flip 'em	with the funky	rhythm I be
kicking. Mu-	sician, in-	flicting compo-	*sition of*
pain. I'm like	Scarface	*sniffing co-*	*caine*, holding a
M-six-	*teen*. See, with the	*pen I'm ex-*	*treme*, now . . .

The first two bars are linked by the compound rhymes, "monkey flip 'em," "funky rhythm," "I be kicking," "musician," "inflicting," and "composition" (highlighted in the diagram), while the next two bars are joined with the compound rhymes, "-sition of pain," "sniffing cocaine," "M-sixteen," and "pen I'm extreme" (shown in italics).

You'll see that the transition from one rhyme scheme to the next is done using a phrase that contains half of the compound rhyme of the first scheme and half of the compound rhyme of the second scheme—this is the "compo*sition of pain*" part, where "composition" is part of the first scheme and "-sition of pain" is part of the second scheme, with "-sition" being part of both schemes. This makes the transition from one scheme to the next seamless.

This level of intricacy with rhyming can be challenging and can make writing verses a lot more difficult and time-consuming. However, this is often part of the appeal of writing them—accepting the challenge and figuring out detailed rhyme patterns.

Ill Bill

That's what we do, as MCs—it can be challenging at times, [but] I think that's what makes it interesting, that's why I love doing it so much. There's a challenge to it, the challenge to be as creative as possible and try to make some words rhyme that might not necessarily fit into place—make that round piece fit into that square hole.

Overlapping Rhyme Schemes

Another way of intertwining rhyme schemes is for one rhyme scheme to overlap into the next scheme. This can be seen on Notorious B.I.G.'s song "Ready to Die" (00:48):

1	2	3	4
I got	techniques	dripping out my	buttcheeks,
sleep on my	stomach so I don't	fuck up my	sheets.
Huh, my shit is	deep,	deeper than my	grave, G.
I'm ready to	die and	nobody can	save me.

In these four bars there are two rhyme schemes—the first covers three bars with the rhymes, "-niques," "cheeks," "sleep," "sheets," "deep," and "deep" again (highlighted in the diagram). The second rhyme scheme joins the last two bars with the rhymes, "grave G" and "save me" (in italics). As we can see, the first rhyme scheme runs quite far into the second rhyme scheme, creating an overlapping scheme. This is also done when compound rhymes overrun into other bars, as shown in the first *How to Rap*, pp. 108–109.

End of One Rhyme Scheme into the
First Line of the Next

One rhyme scheme can be smoothly transitioned into the next by rhyming the last word of the rhyme scheme with the first words of the next line. This example is from Snoop Dogg's lyrics on Dr. Dre's "Fuck Wit Dre Day (And Everybody's Celebrating)" (01:42):

1	2	3	4
Bow wow	wow yippee	yo yippee	yay. The
sound of a	dog brings me	to another	day.
Play	with my	bone, would you,	Timmy? It
seems like you're	good for making	jokes about your	Jimmy.

The first rhyme scheme is a couplet with "yay" and "day," and the second rhyme scheme is a couplet with "Timmy" and "Jimmy." The last rhyme of the first scheme, "day" is immediately rhymed with "play" on the very next line. When listened to, this makes a very smooth transition from the end of the first scheme, going into the next line where the next rhyme scheme starts.

MURS

It's almost like playing a video game to me, because it's all about patterns and fitting things [together].

Popular Couplet Rhyme Placement Patterns

Couplets are the most common type of rhyme scheme and the most common way to use a couplet is to use the first line as the set-up and the second line as a punch line to that set-up. Because of this, there are many forms of this kind of punch-line couplet (punch lines are explained further in *How to Rap*, p. 58).

Although there are almost endless possibilities in the variations, combinations, placements, and patterns that couplets can have, there are several common techniques that sound particularly effective and are used by many MCs.

Alternating Rhymes On and Off the 4 Beat

A popular structure is to have a rhyme fall directly on the 4 beat of the first bar, and then fall on the offbeat of the 4 beat on the second bar. If there is a punch line on the second bar, this usually makes it sound more hard-hitting.

Here is an example from Kool G Rap's "Executioner Style" (00:13), which uses the technique often throughout the song:

1	2	3	4
playground, I	lays down my	laws at the	door, and any
nigga that's looking for	trouble gots to	face these silver	double fours . . .

In the first bar, "door" falls directly on the 4 beat, while in the second bar, the rhyming word "fours" falls on the offbeat of the 4. This way of rhyming is used a lot on Big L's album *Lifestylez Ov Da Poor & Dangerous*, and it is one of the most effective ways of rhyming while using punch lines. This is because it really strongly emphasizes the second bar, where the punch line is normally placed, by creating a variation in placement that can clearly be heard.

Although not used as often, this can be set up the opposite way, such as on the very beginning of Big Daddy Kane's "Set It Off" (00:01):

1	2	3	4
Let it roll,	get bold,	I just	can't hold
back or	fold 'cause I'm the	man with	soul in con- . . .

Here, the first bar has the rhyming word "hold" on the offbeat of the 4, while the second bar has the rhyming word "soul" falling squarely on the 4 beat.

Often, the rhyme placement will make a clever line hit even harder if it is in a pattern that emphasizes the rhymes in different ways—in this way, you can combine the content and the flow so that they support each other.

Myka 9, Freestyle Fellowship

Back in the old school days if you were to battle, you could win a battle not just by what we call "joke rapping" or "bag rapping" [with lots of punch lines and jokes about the other person], you could win a battle by the stylistic expression of your communication—you could win a battle by having a better command of the English language. Nowadays most of the battles revolve around jokes that happen to rhyme, and limited styles, because people are more concerned with the punch line versus a rhyme pattern that punches.

Multiple Rhymes in the First Bar, One Rhyme in the Second Bar

In this popular technique, the first bar will have several rhymes within it, but then the second bar will only have one rhyming element, at the end of the bar. This means that there is a strong emphasis on rhyme, but with plenty of variation due to the non-rhyming parts of the second bar.

The final verse on Snoop Dogg's "Pump, Pump" (02:30) uses this technique in several of its couplets, such as this one:

1	2	3	4
C of the	**year**, you	**hear** and you	**fear**. I got
something for them	**nig**gas in the	**front** and the	**rear**.

The first bar has the rhymes "year," "hear," and "fear," which then only rhymes once at the end of the second bar, with the word "rear."

A very popular addition to this structure is to add an extra rhyme in the second bar—a different rhyme that doesn't rhyme with the main rhyme scheme. For example, here are lyrics from Redman's "Whateva Man" (00:52):

1	2	3	4
	What I **clap** lyri-	**cal**ly tap	**call** back fe-
rocious,	**caus**ing coma-	*toses* to col-	**lapse** . . .

The highlighted syllables show the main rhyme scheme, with "clap," "tap," and "back" rhyming in the first bar and only "-lapse" rhyming in the second bar, at the end of it. The extra rhymes are added in the second bar and are in italics, where "-rocious" rhymes with "-toses."

This is another pattern that is often used for presenting punch lines—it gives enough rhyme and variation to make the lines interesting, while staying simple enough that the content is still easily understood by the listener.

Big Noyd

[With the song, "Things Done Changed,"] that one was kind of easy—if you listen to the rhymes, each line is like a punch line. When you're writing a song like that, it's kinda easier, because you're just really punch-lining it, but it also came out as a concept, [so that tied it all together as well]. Once I got the first four bars, it was downhill from there.

Rhymes on the 2 and the 4 Beats

Another standard and popular placement of rhymes is on the 2 and the 4 beats. Here is an example of this from House of Pain's "Jump Around" (01:18):

1	2	3	4
Word to your	**moms**. I	**came** to drop	**bombs**. I
got more	**rhymes** than the	**Bible's** got	**psalms**. And . . .

The rhymes are "Moms," "bombs," "rhymes" (which is said by bending the word so that it rhymes with the others), and "psalms."

Using rhyme placement such as this means you will automatically write double the number of rhymes than you would if there were only rhymes on the 4 beat—therefore, thinking about rhyme placement can also lead to deciding how many rhymes there will be in each bar.

Rah Digga

From [the song] "Curtains" (00:47), I said, "Be in *San Juan*, on the carriage like I'm *Cam'Ron*, brother trying to chew my *tampon*, with my *pants on*." With an extra couple of minutes of thinking, I've got four words rhyming instead of two, instead of [just] the last two words.

An interesting way to adapt this rhyme scheme is to place a non-rhyming word on the first 4 beat. This is done on the opening lyrics of Cypress Hill's "Insane in the Brain" (00:23):

1	2	3	4
one on the	**flam-**	**boy**ant	*tip* I just
toss that	**ham** in the	**fry**ing	**pan** like . . .

Here, "flam-," "ham," and "pan," all rhyme, with the word "tip" (in italics on the first bar) breaking the pattern, making the rhymes harder to predict and therefore more surprising. We will look at more ways to break patterns later in this book (p. 181).

Rhymes on the 3 and the 4 Beats

Rhymes can also alternate on the 3 and 4 beats. This is an example from LL Cool J's "Mama Said Knock You Out" (00:28):

1	2	3	4
Don't you	**dare**	**stare**,	**you** better
move.		Don't	ever com-	**pare** . . .

The first bar has its final rhyming word on the 3 beat with "stare," which then rhymes with "-pare" on the 4 beat of the second bar. This technique is used frequently throughout the song.

The opposite of this is often used to end a verse or a segment of a verse, as it makes the final line shorter, which is an easy-to-hear signal for the listener that a verse, or a segment of a verse, is finishing. This is done on Eric B. & Rakim's "My Melody" (00:26):

1	2	3	4
M not like the	**rest** of them, I'm	**not** on a	**list**, that's what I'm
saying, I drop	**sci**ence like a	**scien**tist.	My melo- . . .

This couplet rhymes "list" in the first bar on the 4 beat with "-tist" in the second bar on the offbeat of the 3 beat. This shortens the second line and gives the effect of a conclusion or ending of a section.

Rhymes on the 1 and 4 Beats of the Second Bar

This technique is used on LL Cool J's "Mama Said Knock You Out" (01:01), in which the rhyme that would normally fall on the 4 beat of the first bar is moved to the 1 beat of the second bar, then rhymed with another syllable on the 4 beat of the same bar. Here is an example:

1	2	3	4
I'm gonna	**take** this	**it**ty bitty	**world** by
storm	and I'm	**just** getting	**warm**.

This is different from "single liners" in the first *How to Rap* (p. 100), as it is actually just a couplet with the rhyme from the first bar shifted onto the second bar rather than a new rhyme scheme that works on only one bar, as with single liners.

Deciding on exact rhyme placement often involves writing the rest of the lyrics around certain rhyming words or phrases that are in particular predetermined places.

2Mex, The Visionaries

Let's say the sentence has 10 words in it, but the word that rhymes is word number eight. So it's like I need to create the most clever sentence possible in which word number eight is [the rhyming word]. It has to fit in that pocket—it's kind of like a math thing. I kind of mathematically build [the rhyme].

More Complex Extra Rhymes

As we saw in the first *How to Rap* (pp. 103–104), alongside the main rhyme schemes that link bars together, you can also have extra rhymes. Normally these are just a small number of incidental rhymes that occur as one-offs throughout and don't give a structure to the verse. However, they can sometimes become more complex, form patterns of their own, and continue throughout a verse.

They will continue to be just extra rhymes, though, even if they get more complex, as long as there are stronger, more obvious rhyme schemes going on that are the dominant, primary rhyme schemes.

The Dominant, Main Rhyme Schemes

A clear example of this is in Jay-Z's "22 Twos" (00:40). Here is his first verse with just the main rhyme schemes shown and the rest of the words replaced by dashes. These rhyme schemes are the most obvious, dominant rhyme schemes—they are mostly made with compound rhymes, they tend to fall directly on the beats of the bars, and they often fall near the end of the bars, on or around the 4 beat. All these elements make them easy to hear immediately when listening:

1	2	3	4
	--- ---- ---- ----- ----	**lick**ing ---	--- ----
------ -- -	**mis**sion ----- ---	---- ---	- ----dition
	--- ---- ----- ------	------- - ---	-- --spicions ----
----- ---- -	**fish** in - ----- --	------ -----	listen
	--- ---- ------- ----- --	**la**dies --	-- --- -

--- ---	--- --- - ---	--- ----	------- --- shady
--- ---- **la**dies ---- -----		------ ---	---- *chances*
--- ---- -------- -------		------ ----	---- ----- --*mance is*
--- ---- ------- ----- --		---- --- ----	------ --
vances	-- --------	---- ---	--- ---- *answers*
- ----- - ----- ---- BLOCK		TOO MANY	**TIMES**
ROCKED TOO MANY	**RHYMES**	**COCKED** TOO MANY	**NINES**
--- -- --- --	-------- -- ----	--- ---- --	---- together
----- --- ---- ----- --- --- ----		---- -	---- forever
- ---- ------- ---		**guide**lines -----	--- ----
------ ride	**mine** -- -	------ ------ -----	--- rhymes

There are six main rhyme schemes here. The first four bars are joined by the rhyme of "licking," "mission," "-dition," "-spicions," "fish in," and "listen." The next two bars are linked by "ladies" and "shady," and this also briefly runs into a third bar with "ladies." In the same bar, a new scheme starts, joining four bars with "chances," "-mance is," "-vances," and "answers." The final three rhyme schemes are all couplets, each joining together two bars. The first couplet is joined by "block too many times," "rocked too many rhymes," and "cocked too many nines"; the second is joined by "together" and "forever"; and the final couplet is joined by "guidelines," "ride mine," and "rhymes."

The Extra Rhymes Pattern

Here is the same verse from Jay-Z's "22 Twos," except this time with the pattern of extra rhymes shown and highlighted. This extra rhyme pattern is a lot subtler than the main rhyme schemes and is harder to hear if you're not listening for it, even though it runs throughout the verse. This is because it has the opposite characteristics—the rhymes are all single syllables (no compound rhymes), they mostly fall on offbeats of the bars (rather than prominently on the beats of the bars), and they rarely fall near the end of the bars (so they are rarely a rhyme that a line or punch line ends on):

1	2	3	4
Too ----	---- ----- ----	------- ---	too ----
------- -- -	------- ----- ---	---- ---	- ---------
too ----	----- -------	------- - ---	-- ---------- ----
----- ----- -	---- -- - ---- --	------ -----	------
too ----	------- ----- --	------- --	-- --- -
--- ---	--- --- - ---	too ----	------- --- -----
too ----	------ ---- -----	------ too	---- -------
too ----	-------- -------	------ ----	---- ---- ------- --
too ----	------- ----- --	---- too ----	------- --
------	-- --------	---- ---	too ---- -------
- ---- -	----- ---- -----	too ----	-----
------	too ----	------	too ----	-----
too to --- --	-------- -- ----	too ---- to	---- --------
----- too ----	----- --- too ----	---- -	---- -------
- ---- ------	---	---------- -----	too ----
------ ----	---- -- -	------ ------ -----	two ------

The actual title and content of the song draws attention to this pattern of extra rhymes—the "22 Twos" of the title are the words "to," "too," and "two" that run throughout the verse. Normally, however, there won't be as clear a reference to the extra rhymes as there is in this track. But they can usually be heard on some level by the listener, because there will be a lot more words rhyming overall and this adds to the general sound of the verse.

This level of intricacy in the rhyming patterns often requires a more precise notational system in order to keep track of the details.

Vinnie Paz, Jedi Mind Tricks

I'm pretty [particular] about the way that it's written—it's pretty neat and it's pretty much lined out the way I want to rhyme it. I've seen other people's rhyme books and I don't know how the fuck you even know what you're doing. [It's] funny to see everybody else's process, it's pretty interesting. But yeah, it's pretty well organized [with me]—it's bar by bar.

Adding complexity to the rhymes works for some MCs, but often it can be just as good to stand out in a different area, as hip-hop already has a number of MCs whose main focus is adding more and more rhymes.

Speech, Arrested Development

I love artists that are really just all about the rhyme, but I just know where I fit in, and to me every artist has to know that, they gotta know where they fit into the scheme of hip-hop and get into the genre of the music and know what they're offering and why is it special and feel comfortable with that. You can't be every type of artist, you gotta be who you are.

Breaking Patterns

Most rhyming techniques and rhyme schemes are concerned with creating patterns in one way or another—creating links through the repetition of certain sounds. However, if a pattern is carried on for a long time, or if all the patterns are easy for the listener to guess, then it may become too predictable, as there is no element of surprise or variation.

A good way to create unpredictability and surprise, to keep the listener interested, is to first create a pattern and then break it. This can be done with the type of rhyme used, nonrhyming words or phrases, the placement of rhyme, or the number of rhymes.

Tajai, Souls of Mischief

Raps are kind of like puzzles, so you get into a sort of pattern and then once you get into that pattern you look for a way out of that pattern.

Switching to Different Types of
Rhyme to Break a Pattern

A good way to break a pattern of rhyme is to suddenly introduce a different type of rhyme that sounds noticeably different, but still has some elements of the previous pattern.

This technique is done on Naughty by Nature's "Feel Me Flow" (00:37) with the line:

> . . . full of Phillies and rallies, suckers get silly as Sally, then found in alleys. I'm rowdy, really.

The pattern of rhyme was created with compound rhymes that include "Phillies and rallies" and "silly as Sally," but then it ends with "alleys," "rowdy," and "really." So instead of continuing the same format of compound rhymes right to the end, it ends with three words that break the more obvious pattern, but with elements that still rhyme in a different way ("alleys" is partially rhymed with the main compound rhymes, and "rowdy" and "really" use consonance to link both of them together—partial rhyming and consonance are explained in the first *How to Rap*, pp. 91 and 87).

The "e" sound in the middle of "really" makes that word sound the most unexpected when you listen to the verse—as a strong "e" sound had not been used throughout the rest of the rhyme scheme up until then.

Techniques such as this can often be done using nonsensical combinations of words—if the sound of the technique is interesting and surprising enough, understandable content is not always needed.

Myka 9, Freestyle Fellowship

It's kinda gibberish if you're just writing and putting stuff down that you don't really understand, but even in that sense, gibberish is a style. There's many different styles to the form—we call that wild style, where you're just putting random words together because you like the way the syllables and the consonants ring.

Using Nonrhyming Words to Break a Pattern

Another good way to break up a pattern of rhyme is to suddenly introduce a nonrhyming word or line that doesn't fit in with the rest of the rhyme scheme.

This is done on Cypress Hill's "Hole in the Head" (00:37) on the lines:

1	2	3	4
Booyaa,	**spit**ting out	**buck**shots.	**Boy** me say
blood clot,		*so* **you** *can call a*	*pig.*

The highlighted words show the rhyme from the first bar to the second, but the second bar ends with the phrase, "so you can call a pig" (shown in italics). This phrase doesn't rhyme with the previous or subsequent lines, even though the word "pig" falls clearly and strongly on the 4 beat, suggesting that it should rhyme with something, but it is nonrhyming. This makes the phrase stand out and become more distinct, because it is surrounded by patterns of rhyme but is not part of one itself.

Chuck D, Public Enemy

Sometimes you don't have to rhyme. Sometimes you can write something profound and not rhyme the word.

Short, Emphasized Nonrhyming Phrase

This is sometimes done with a short, nonrhyming phrase that is shouted, to give it emphasis, so it stands out even more as a nonrhyming break of the pattern. This is done by Snoop Dogg at the end of Dr. Dre's "Day the Niggaz Took Over" (04:24):

1	2	3	4
Blam	blam,	blam till them	fall.
Listen to the	shots from the	nigga Doggy	Dogg, *bidda bye!*

In this example, the two bars are linked by the rhyme of "fall" with "Dogg" (by bending the sounds, as described in the first *How to Rap*, p. 85), and then the short phrase "bidda bye" is said louder and doesn't rhyme with anything else—so the nonrhyming words are suddenly and abruptly introduced, surprising the listener and breaking up the pattern as a kind of loud, non-rhyming addition.

Big Noyd

Sometimes you want to say something that don't rhyme, but that [can be] the most creative part. Sometimes you come across something [like] that—I say it even if it don't rhyme.

Bootie Brown, The Pharcyde

I don't think it's necessary, like you have to rhyme. I don't think that's even a requirement.

Nonrhyming Phrase to End a Verse

A popular way to use this technique is for a nonrhyming phrase to lead into the chorus or a new verse by another MC, after the final rhyme. This is done by 2Pac on "Dear Mama" when he says, "You are appreciated" as the last line of the verse—the phrase doesn't rhyme with anything else, but signals that the chorus is beginning. He also does this on his song "Definition of a Thug Nigga," at the end of the first and final verses, with the phrase "My definition of a thug nigga." This is also done by Method Man on Wu-Tang Clan's "Triumph" (01:47):

1	2	3	4
Guns of	**Navarone**	**tear**ing up your	**battle** zone
rip through your	**slums** . . .		

Here, the first line in the diagram has a single-liner rhyme (*How to Rap*, p. 100, describes single-liners) with the rhymes "Navarone" and "battle zone." The verse finishes with a non-rhyming phrase, "rip through your slums," just before the next MC's verse starts.

Bobby Creekwater

I never limit myself to just having to rhyme every line—sometimes it might not rhyme, the important thing is to get your point across, I think.

Changing the Placement of Rhymes to Break Patterns

A common way to break patterns is to first create a pattern in which rhyming words continually fall in the same place in the bars of music—for example, they could fall on the 4 beat of each bar for several bars. Then, to break the pattern, the rhyming words can suddenly start appearing in different places in the bar, on the 3 beat for example. This keeps the listener guessing, as they expect a rhyme in a certain place, but then they are surprised when it appears in a different place.

This type of unexpected rhyme placement is a large part of Method Man's rhyme style. Below are the main three rhyme schemes on Method Man's verse on "Shame on a Nigga" (00:51). The words that are not part of these rhyme schemes have been replaced with dashes, so that you can see the rhyme schemes more clearly and where the words fall in the flow diagram:

1	2	3	4
--- --	razor	--- -- ---- ---	major ---
------ --	---- -----	----- -- --	flavor
-------	------ ------	at ya	----- -- -----
--- -- ----- -	--- -- -	gat ya	--- ----- -----
capture ---	------ ---	stature ---	----- --- ---
rapture	--- ------ --	------- ----	mastered
-- -----	*never* -	--- --- -------	---- -- ---
---- --- --	*terror*	----- ----- -	*sever* ---
---- ---- ---	---------- --	*better* ----	-- ---*petor*
--- ---- ---	*petitor* ----	*ever* ----	--- --*gether*

The verse is 10 bars long. The first rhyme scheme starts out with a very standard rhyme placement for the first two bars—"razor" falls on the 2 beat, then "major" and "flavor" both fall on the 4 beat. However, this is where the regular, predictable pattern of placement ends.

The second rhyme scheme (which is highlighted) begins on the third bar, but it breaks the first pattern of placement, because it starts on the 3 beat instead, with "at ya." It continues this pattern of appearing on the 3 beat for the next couple of bars with "gat ya" and "stature," but then the pattern is broken again with "mastered" falling on the 4 beat. A short pattern of the same rhyme scheme falling on the 1 beat happens with "capture" and "rapture," which again is unpredictably placed and is soon broken again.

The third rhyme scheme (shown in italics) starts another pattern—it appears on the 2 beat with "never," and it appears again on the 2 beat with "terror." This pattern is broken with the placement then falling around the 4 beat for the rest of the verse with "sever," "-petor," and "-gether," as well as the 3 beat for the last couple of lines with "better" and "ever," and a brief appearance on the 2 beat again for the final line, "-petitor."

In each of the three rhyme schemes, a pattern is created, then broken, then replaced by a new rhyme scheme. This keeps the listener guessing, as patterns they expect to continue are suddenly broken.

Wise Intelligent, Poor Righteous Teachers

It's hard for me to just be one way all the time on a track, so I try to keep it fresh, keep it hip-hop, keep bringing something different to the table, make sure I'm bringing a different rhyme flow. I definitely make a conscious effort to come up with a different flow.

Rhyme Schemes That Last for an Odd Number of Bars

Normally, rhyme schemes last for an even number of bars—so the most common lengths of rhyme schemes are two, four, six, and eight bars. So an unpredictable way to use rhyme schemes is to make them join together an odd number of bars—one-, three-, five-, and seven-bar rhyme schemes. The listener is used to hearing even numbers of bars being joined together, so it is surprising when a rhyme scheme lasts for an odd number—it sounds like the rhyme scheme has changed before it has reached its natural conclusion.

An example of this is on KRS-One's final verse of "MCs Act Like They Don't Know" (03:37):

1	2	3	4
---- ---- -- ---	--- ---- Is ----	---- I --	rive
wide -----	fied live	like --- -----	tide
--- ---- ---	lied	I --side	like ----
----- -- ---	----- side -- ---	------ --------	fied
------ ------ ---	-------- ---	--- --- hide	------ ---- --
----- -----	nism --- --	---- -- ----	------- ----
cism	-- - ------ ---		ism ---
-------- ------	--- -------	------ ---- -	give 'em.

The first rhyme scheme is created with assonance, using an "i" sound in words and syllables such as "live," "like," "tide," and "-fied." This rhyme scheme continues for five bars, at which point it switches to the second rhyme scheme, rhyming "-nism" with "-cism," "-ism," and "give 'em."

This second rhyme scheme that ends the verse is an odd number of bars long (three bars), due to the one before it also lasting for an odd number of bars (five bars). The listener expects a regular, even number of bars, so when the sixth bar of the example starts a new rhyme scheme instead of completing the one before it, it's unexpected and surprising.

Also, the single-liner rhyme scheme described in the first *How to Rap* (p. 100) is a great technique for breaking up other, longer rhyme scheme patterns, as it creates a short rhyme scheme on just a single bar, resulting in an odd number of bars that rhyme.

Imani, The Pharcyde

Really, in the field of music, it's timing for me, and it's mathematical. You [can hear] if everything goes in four bars, four bars, four bars. People's minds are trained and programmed to listen [and] to like certain things for certain reasons, and math has a lot to do with why you like certain shit—I think because it's even and it's balanced. But sometimes I like to break it outside the box, because why does it have to be like that? Everybody has done it that way over the years, but it doesn't have to be like that. You can make any kind of [pattern]. Though that doesn't mean people gonna like it!

Changing the Number of Rhymes in a Bar to Break Patterns

Another way to be unpredictable is to create a pattern in which you rhyme a lot of words in each bar and then suddenly rhyme only a few, or the other way around—rhyme few words per bar, then suddenly rhyme many ("Number of Rhymes in a Bar" is explained in the first *How to Rap*, p. 104).

This is done in R.A. the Rugged Man's song "Chains" (01:22), in which he begins his verse with relatively few rhymes per bar, continuing until he reaches the section that begins "Hospitable, hittable, cooler than Digable . . ."—rapping many rhymes in each bar. This is a sudden change that is surprising for the listener. He then ends the verse with a couple of bars with few rhymes again, to keep it unpredictable.

Again, adding a run of compound rhymes often means sacrificing some content, so breaking a pattern in this way may also mean shifting the topic to a more abstract and less literal form of content.

Royce Da 5′9″

Back in the day, I used to rhyme a bunch of big words and people used to love me for that, like at the open mics, and they didn't necessarily make sense. It wasn't like I was just saying a bunch of words, but I'd say two bars and the lines in that two bars would make sense with each other, but then the next two bars would just be about something else. It'd be like scatterbrain, all over the place, and just abstract.

Three-Bar Loops

Usually, hip-hop beats feature loops that repeat either one bar of music over and over, or two bars, or four bars.

Examples of one-bar loops are GZA's "Shadowboxing" and Cypress Hill's "Insane in the Brain," as the main loops in these songs last for one bar before looping and starting again.

Examples of two-bar loops are songs such as Wu-Tang Clan's "C.R.E.A.M," in which the main loop has a piano melody that lasts for two bars before restarting, and Cypress Hill's "Hits from the Bong," in which the melody also lasts for two bars.

Examples of four-bar loops are Snoop Dogg's "Gz & Hustlaz," in which the main piano melody lasts for four bars before it begins again, and A Tribe Called Quest's "Excursions," in which the bassline pattern covers four bars before starting again.

These are common loops in which the music "restarts" in an obvious, predictable place, so if the rhymes are unpredictable it provides a contrast. Or if a more predictable pattern of rhymes is used, it will line up with the predictable pattern of the music.

However, some hip-hop beats use an odd number of bars before the music repeats. Usually this is done with a three-bar loop. There are still four beats in each bar (unlike with 3/4 beats, which is covered in the "Rhythm" chapter of this book, p. 53), but there are three bars of music before it repeats itself.

Songs with three-bar loops include De La Soul's "Stakes Is High" and Dilated Peoples' "Worst Comes to Worst." With "Worst Comes to Worst," Evidence of Dilated Peoples notes that because the music of the song repeats itself in an unusual place, due to its three-bar loop, it meant that lyrics had to be written specifically for it, in order to make it sound correct.

Evidence, Dilated Peoples

Most rap beats [repeat their pattern after an even number of bars, but "Worst Comes to Worst"] was different. So we couldn't use words or the pattern that we already had, we had to actually script it to the beat, because it turned around in an odd place.

This normally involves altering the rhyme scheme so that it uses either multi-liners (described in *How to Rap*, p. 101) that last for three bars or a couplet followed by a single-liner to fit into the three-bar loop structure provided by the music. If a rhyme scheme is used that involves even numbers of bars, such as couplets or four-bar multi-liner rhyme schemes, then it will often sound strange, as the music will be restarting but the rhyme scheme won't be.

Wise Intelligent, Poor Righteous Teachers

I'll choose a beat [and] I'm consciously listening for tracks and saying, "Nah, they wouldn't rap to this, nobody would rhyme to this track, so I'm gonna rhyme to it," and it challenges me to create a flow for that particular beat.

Crooked I

To me, every instrumental has a secret way to ride that certain beat, you just have to unlock it. Each beat needs to be listened to, and you've got to really sit back and think, "Now how am I gonna ride this beat," to make it sound better, to keep it interesting.

Royce Da 5'9"

I don't like using the same flow. I like my flows to match that particular beat that it's gonna be on.

Poetry Terms Versus Rapping Terms: A Note on Terminology

This section is a note on the terms used to describe some of the techniques used in How to Rap *and* How to Rap 2. *You do not need to be familiar with these terms to use the techniques in the two books, but it is helpful if you want to further understand how some of the techniques are described.*

Sometimes, rap rhymes are described using terms from traditional poetry. This can be useful in some cases, such as with assonance and consonance (used in the first *How to Rap*, pp. 84, 86). However, some of the terms are less useful. The two most generally misused and inaccurate terms are *end rhymes* and *internal rhymes*. In poetry, these terms are very accurate and precise. However, they can be misleading when talking about rap's rhymes.

End Rhymes

In poetry, *end rhymes* are rhymes that fall at the end of a line — which is very easy to identify in poetry, because it is written down on the page and a line either ends with a rhyming word or it doesn't. But in rapping, there is no clear "end" of a line. In fact, there are no obvious "lines" either, as the words are set to bars of music. Since it isn't clear where a bar ends (as we will see), and the term "end rhyme" relies on there being a clear end, it makes the term inaccurate.

The closest type of rap rhyme to poetry's end rhyme is a rap couplet in which the rhymes fall on the 4 beat in each bar. Even then, there are very often more words after the 4 beat but on the same bar, as in this example from LL Cool J's "I Can't Live Without My Radio" (00:10):

1	2	3	4
radio, be-	**lieve** me, I	**like** it	**loud**. *I'm the*
man with a	**box** that can	**rock** the	**crowd**. *Walking . . .*

The couplet is placed on the 4 beat with the rhymes "loud" and "crowd," but these rhymes don't actually end the bar of music— the words "I'm the" end the first bar, and the word "walking" ends the second bar.

Alternatively, you might have a rhyme that occurs on the off-beat of the 4 beat, as in this example from Jay-Z's "22 Twos" (00:46):

1	2	3	4
	Too many **rough** mother-	**fuck**ers, I got	**my** suspicions that
you're just a	**fish** in a pool of	**sharks**, nigga,	listen.

Here, the bars are joined by the rhyming of "-spicions" and "listen." These rhymes are placed on the offbeat of the 4, with "-spicions" surrounded by other syllables and "listen" as the last word on the bar. This complicates the term "end rhyme," as now it is not clear if the "end" is on the 4 beat or after the 4 beat, or if it is the last word of the bar.

A couplet's rhymes might not even appear near the 4 beat at all. They may appear on the 3 beat, for example, as in Method Man's verse on Wu-Tang Clan's "Shame on a Nigga" (00:56):

1	2	3	4
Gunning,	**com**ing coming	**at** ya.	**First** I'm gonna
get ya, once I	**got** ya I	**gat** ya.	**You** could never . . .

The couplet rhyme of "at ya" and "gat ya" joins the two bars together and could be said to effectively "end" the "line" on the 3 beat. So again, the term "end rhyme" loses meaning when talking about rapping, because you can essentially "end" anywhere in the bar—there is no clear, stable end point.

In poetry, the end of a line never changes—it is the last word in a line, written on paper. But rap lyrics are set to bars of music, not lines on the page, and it is usually unclear where the end of a bar is, making the term "end rhyme" problematic.

Internal Rhyme

As rap lyrics are set to bars of music and not written in clearly identifiable "lines," and because it is not clear where the end of a bar is, the term "internal rhyme" is inaccurate as well.

In poetry, internal rhymes are rhymes that are placed within the lines, rather than at the ends of them. But with rapping, if it is not clear where the end point is in a bar, all the rhymes could be described as "internal," making the term meaningless.

The rough equivalent to internal rhyme in rapping, and what people are normally referring to when they mention internal rhyme in rap, is how some MCs add more rhymes in each bar (as we saw earlier with "Runs of Rhyme," p. 160, and in *How to Rap*, p. 104), the use of extra rhymes (p. 178, and in *How to Rap*, p. 103), and the use of compound rhymes to add more rhyming sounds to a verse (*How to Rap*, pp. 87–91).

Rapping Terms

In rapped rhymes, it is more accurate to describe the type of rhyme (*How to Rap*, pp. 82–91), the type of rhyme scheme (*How to Rap*, p. 99), the placement of the rhymes (*How to Rap*, p. 107), how many rhymes there are in a bar (*How to Rap*, p. 104), and if there are extra rhymes (*How to Rap*, p. 103).

This is because these terms accurately describe what is going on with the rhymes and rhyme schemes in rap lyrics, as opposed to terms created for a different art form that are then applied to the art form of rapping.

4

Enunciation Rudiments

Never think that there is some grand oasis that you will
reach where you don't have to work anymore—it don't
exist. You can always stand to improve upon yourself,
and that's good game on life or rapping.
◂ Del the Funky Homosapien ▸

In the first *How to Rap*, MCs with fast rapping styles such as Twista,
Dray of Das EFX, and Gift of Gab of Blackalicious explained how
they learned to rap quickly and clearly by practicing saying lyrics over and over, often memorizing whole verses to repeat constantly until they could say all the words fluidly (*How to Rap*, pp.
245, 246, 269–270).

And several fast rappers, such as Tech N9ne and E-40, explain
in this book and the previous one how they learned fast rhythms
and delivery by mimicking drums and percussion (p. 3 and *How
to Rap*, p. 111).

These two elements—repeated practice and mimicking drumming—form the basis of this part of the book, helping you to
develop and master enunciation.

Royce Da 5'9"

You just gotta keep working at it, man. You become a better
MC just like you become a better anything—practice makes
perfect, that applies to anything you want to get good at.
You gotta start somewhere. It's just like getting in the gym

and working out, when you get in there you might only be able to bench press a quarter on each side of the bar, six weeks later, you'll be doing 225 [lbs]. You just gotta stay at it and you just gotta work, practice makes perfect. Keep practicing and you'll get good at it.

Basic Enunciation Guidelines

Drum Rudiments

When learning to play drums, percussionists practice a set of "drum rudiments" that range from basic patterns—such as hitting a drum with your right hand, then your left hand, and then repeating that over and over—to more complex patterns.

As well as helping them learn the different rhythmic patterns, drum rudiments help them to physically become more skillful at performing the techniques, by increasing the speed while keeping the precision. By practicing these rudiments repeatedly, the drummer masters all the individual elements. There are a set of "40 International Drum Rudiments" that are standard for drummers to practice.

Enunciation Rudiments

In the same way, fast rappers have continually practiced saying different combinations of sounds over and over, until they reach the point at which they can rap effectively at different speeds, all with the highest level of clarity and control. This often comes from repeating the lyrics of other MCs, as well as from a love of words and sounds in general.

Mr. Lif

It started for me just from being a fan, listening to Run DMC, Chubb Rock, LL Cool J, all those groups back in the day. Loving their songs and naturally following along with the lyrics, just not really realizing that I was teaching myself how to rhyme—just being able to keep up with them, that's where the verbal dexterity came from. And also my love of the English language, the passion for words just went hand in hand with what I had learned.

To help with this method of learning, *How to Rap 2* provides you with a list of enunciation rudiments. These are a collection of lines of lyrics from notable MCs that go through every sound in the English language. These can be repeated individually until you can say them all clearly at a fast speed. Practicing these rudiments will allow you to rap any lyrics at fast speeds without stumbling or losing clarity on the microphone.

Enunciation is especially important for keeping in time if you plan on rapping fast, either as a main style or by including fast sections in your raps to add variety to the flow. MCs who use a large number of compound rhymes, such as Kool G Rap, Big Daddy Kane, Eminem, and Big Pun, need flawless enunciation as well, since lyrics that have a lot of rhymes can be tricky to perform, often mimicking tongue twisters. Clarity through enunciation is also very important for MCs with strong content in their lyrics—for example, stories need to be clearly rapped to be followed and understood.

Andy Cat, Ugly Duckling

For me, it was memorizing raps before I ever really started writing them, and reciting them back. I remember going to great trouble sometimes to try and figure out all the words, so I could properly deliver the rap exactly. I can remember Slick Rick's "Children's Story," trying to figure out every single one of those lines and trying to deliver it the way he did and tell the whole story.

How Often to Practice

As with learning an instrument, it helps to practice often. Most accomplished musicians in every genre practice on an almost daily basis, continually learning and honing their skills.

O.C., Diggin' in the Crates

[I was] just doing it over and over, sitting in my room, especially when I was young, sitting in my room or I was always around [Pharoahe] Monch and Prince Po and other dudes.

Zumbi, Zion I

It's just really spending time with your art—you gotta take it serious and you gotta do it every day, basically, to make it good.

Bishop Lamont

You had to do it every day, it had to be, that was the only way to get better at it. It wasn't like, I'll just do it on Saturdays, but during the week at school . . . nah, we were doing it every day.

Practice doesn't have to be a formal activity in which you set aside a time specifically to do it—even when you're just repeating lines while watching TV, you're practicing. As Cappadonna says, "Every time I do it, to me, is practice, because you know the more you do it, the better you get."

B-Real, Cypress Hill

You want to do all of those things as much as you can, because it builds you up—it builds your skills and it makes you better.

How to Practice the Rudiments

In the first *How to Rap*, both Gift of Gab of Blackalicious and Akir talk about taking an individual line and repeating it over and over (*How to Rap*, pp. 245, 246) in order to build up the speed while keeping the clarity. This is what drummers do as well, to perfect their rhythms at different speeds.

A lot of MCs, therefore, mimic the technique drummers are taught to do and apply it to rapping. The technique with each rudiment is to start off relatively slowly to make sure the words are said clearly, then gradually increase the speed with which you're saying it. Once you reach the point where you're saying it as fast as you can say it, keep repeating it at that speed for a while, then slow back down, in a controlled way so that every syllable is being said precisely at every speed.

The Lady of Rage

That was just something that I practiced. I wanted to enunciate and I wanted to be heard clearly, so when I'm practicing it, I just say it over and over. That's something that I take pride in, and I understand that can go a long way, [a] bigger delivery. I'm a perfectionist—I do it over and over and over until I get it right, until it sounds right to me.

With each sound, it's also helpful to practice it "stuttered" on its own. This helps with overall clarity and precision, and also if you do any rapping involving a stuttering technique, as discussed on p. 115.

T3, Slum Village

I practice all the time. I'd spend a good four or five hours in the basement a day, just doing it over and over again.

How the Rudiments Are Presented

Each of the rudiments is based on one of the sounds in the English language, using a line of lyrics that repeats that sound a lot, as well as giving an example of how the sound can be stuttered. The rudiments are organized in alphabetical order, going through consonant sounds first, followed by vowel sounds.

Each sound is explained first, showing an example of a word with that sound in, underlined. For example if the sound is a "b" sound, the word used is "bed" with the "b" sound in it underlined.

Some of the rudiments use the same letters, but are actually different sounds, such as the "oo" in "book," and the "oo" in "too." They both use an "oo" in how they are written, but it is a different sound produced in each word.

While it is useful to understand the differences between the sounds, it is not essential in order to say them—actually practicing each of the rudiments is the important thing. Each of the sounds normally has a special symbol (as they are part of the International Phonetic Alphabet), but it is clearer here to show them using regular letters, as the symbols make no difference for actually learning enunciation.

Consonant Sounds

B (as in "bed")

Bang bang, the boogie to the boogie, say up jump the boogie, to the bang bang boogie . . .

Example is from: Sugarhill Gang's "Rapper's Delight"
Stutter technique: "buh-buh-buh-buh . . ." repeated

C/K (as in "cat" or "kilo")

Killer cadence can keep me crushing the competition, coming correct when creating the crazy composition . . .

Example is from: Crooked I on Tech N9ne's "Sickology 101"
Stutter technique: "kuh-kuh-kuh-kuh . . ." repeated

CH (as in "church")

Chiggidy check yourself . . .

Example is from: Das EFX on Ice Cube's "Check Yo' Self"
Stutter technique: "chuh-chuh-chuh-chuh . . ." repeated

D (as in "do")

Done did that, done did this, diddle don. Domination don't dignify diction . . .

Example is from: Gift of Gab on Blackalicious's "A2G"
Stutter technique: "duh-duh-duh-duh . . ." repeated

F/PH (as in "five" or "photo")

Focus upon the fact that facts can be fabricated to form lies. My phonetics alone forces feeble MCs into defense on the fly . . .

Example is from: Pharoahe Monch, "Hell"
Stutter technique: "fuh-fuh-fuh-fuh . . ." repeated

G (as in "go")

Get blurred, get nerve, get gone or go home. I'm headed for the rim gonna claim a gold throne . . .

Example is from: MURS on 3 Meloncholy Gypsies' "The Plannit"
Stutter technique: "guh-guh-guh-guh . . ." repeated

H (as in "<u>h</u>ello")

Head hoodlum hitting heads heavenly hypnotizing, hire hit men harness be holding heaters . . .

Example is from: Papoose, "Alphabetical Slaughter"
Stutter technique: "huh-huh-huh-huh . . ." repeated

J (as in "<u>judg</u>e")

Juiced on my jams like Jheri curls jocking joints. Justly, it's just me, writing my journals . . .

Example is from: Gift of Gab on Blackalicious's "Alphabet Aerobics"
Stutter technique: "juh-juh-juh-juh . . ." repeated

L (as in "<u>l</u>ive")

Lower level, lackluster, last, least, limp-lover, lousy, lame, late, lethargic, lazy lemon, little logic . . .

Example is from: Kool Moe Dee on "Let's Go"
Stutter technique: "luh-luh-luh-luh . . ." repeated

M (as in "<u>m</u>ilk")

Music mixed mellow maintains to make melodies for MCs motivates the breaks . . .

Example is from: Rakim, "Follow the Leader"
Stutter technique: "muh-muh-muh-muh . . ." repeated

N (as in "<u>n</u>o")

No, my narratives, not for narcoleptic narcissists. Naive native nitwits natter negative nastiness . . .

Example is from: Lowkey on "Alphabet Assassin"
Stutter technique: "nuh-nuh-nuh-nuh . . ." repeated

NG (as in "si*ng*")

Things, clinging, dreaming, thinking of being Miss Thing, with this ring . . .

Example is from: Tech N9ne, "This Ring"
Stutter technique: "ing-ing-ing-ing . . ." repeated

P (as in "*p*ig")

Peter Piper picked a peck of pickled peppers . . .

Example is from: Run DMC's "Peter Piper," Lil Kim's "Queen Bitch," Rick Ross's "Live Fast, Die Young," Kool G Rap's "Keep It Swingin'," MF Doom's "Impostas," and Big Boi on Outkast's "Red Velvet"
Stutter technique: "puh-puh-puh-puh . . ." repeated

Q (as in "*q*ueen")

Quite quaint quotes keep quiet, it's Quannum. Quarrelers ain't got a quarter . . .

Example is from: Blackalicious's "Alphabet Aerobics"
Stutter technique: "qwuh-qwuh-qwuh-qwuh . . ." repeated

R (as in "*r*ead")

Real renegade rap rebels rip rhymes ferociously . . .

Example is from: KRS-One on Tim Dog's "I Get Wrecked"
Stutter technique: "ruh-ruh-ruh-ruh . . ." repeated

S (as in "*s*ix")

Soul-simulated, sounds from a stocky semi-social, never seem sloppy. See silly slapping suckers . . .

Example is from: Naughty by Nature's "Yoke the Joker"
Stutter technique: "suh-suh-suh-suh . . ." repeated

S (as in "ca_s_ual")

Decisions, decisions, garage looks like Precision Collision . . .

Example is from: Dr. Dre on "Crack a Bottle"
Stutter technique: "zhuh-zhuh-zhuh-zhuh . . ." repeated

SH (as in "_sh_ort")

I'm a sure-shot shooter and I'm the big shot, the big shot . . .

Example is from: Jungle Brothers' "Braggin' and Boastin'"
Stutter technique: "shuh-shuh-shuh-shuh . . ." repeated

T (as in "_t_ime")

Too many nines, too. To all my brothers it ain't too late to come together . . .

Example is from: Jay-Z's "22 Twos"
Stutter technique: "tuh-tuh-tuh-tuh . . ." repeated

TH (as in "_th_ink")

Thorough thug terrifying. Toting two tecs taking, territories thoroughly thriving . . .

Example is from: Papoose, "Alphabetical Slaughter"
Stutter technique: "think-think-think-think . . ." repeated

TH (as in "_th_e")

The T, to the R, to the E, to the A, to the C, to the H is back . . .

Example is from: Treach on South Central Cartel Productions' "Sowhatusayin"
Stutter technique: "the-the-the-the . . ." repeated

V (as in "<u>v</u>ery")

Visualize vocab, victoriously vocalized. Versatile vice-versa verbals viciously victimize . . .

Example is from: Papoose, "Alphabetical Slaughter"
Stutter technique: "vuh-vuh-vuh-vuh . . ." repeated

W (as in "<u>w</u>indow")

If it wasn't here, will she wanna go? You don't wanna ask, but you wanna know . . .

Example is from: Fabolous on "When the Money Goes (Remix)"
Stutter technique: "wuh-wuh-wuh-wuh . . ." repeated

Y (as in "<u>y</u>es")

Yellow back, yak mouth, young ones yaws. Yesterday's lawn yards . . .

Example is from: Blackalicious's "Alphabet Aerobics"
Stutter technique: "yuh-yuh-yuh-yuh . . ." repeated

Z (as in "<u>z</u>oo")

Zig-zag zombies, zooming to the zenith. Zero in Zen thoughts, overzealous rhyme zealots . . .

Example is from: Blackalicious's "Alphabet Aerobics"
Stutter technique: "zuh-zuh-zuh-zuh . . ." repeated

Consonant Combinations

Sometimes consonants are placed together to create a blend of two sounds. For example, "BR" as in "brown" uses the "B" and "R" sounds together. Although these sounds have been covered individually in the previous list, it is good to practice the combinations, as many of them are used frequently.

BL (as in "<u>bl</u>ock")

Half blue and half black, block . . .

Example is from: Apathy's "No Joke"
Stutter technique: "bluh-bluh-bluh-bluh . . ." repeated

BR (as in "<u>br</u>own")

Brother, back to back I slam. Bread and butter, break beats . . .

Example is from: Redman on EPMD's "Hardcore"
Stutter technique: "bruh-bruh-bruh-bruh . . ." repeated

CL (as in "<u>cl</u>ash")

Let the smoke cloud clear . . .

Example is from: Wu-Tang Clan's "Uzi (Pinky Ring)"
Stutter technique: "cluh-cluh-cluh-cluh . . ." repeated

CR (as in "<u>cr</u>ash")

Crooked corrupted criminal crime boss with cream . . .

Example is from: McGruff on Children of the Corn's "American Dream"
Stutter technique: "cruh-cruh-cruh-cruh . . ." repeated

CT (as in "fa<u>ct</u>")

Live and direct, respect it to the underground connect . . .

Example is from: Redman on "On Fire"
Stutter technique: "act-act-act-act . . ." repeated

DR (as in "<u>dr</u>ive")

If you're driving, don't drink and if you drink, don't drive . . .

Example is from: Beastie Boys on "Live at P.J.'s"
Stutter technique: "druh-druh-druh-druh . . ." repeated

FL (as in "<u>fl</u>y")

Not afraid to fly, you need to get on a flight and fly tonight . . .

Example is from: Ja Rule on "Extasy"
Stutter technique: "fluh-fluh-fluh-fluh . . ." repeated

FR (as in "<u>fr</u>og")

French eyes and with French fries and French thighs . . .

Example is from: Snoop Dogg on "Mission Cleopatra"
Stutter technique: "fruh-fruh-fruh-fruh . . ." repeated

FT (as in "le<u>ft</u>")

The gift that can lift the myth that is swift . . .

Example is from: Masta Ace on Marley Marl's "Simon Says"
Stutter technique: "ift-ift-ift-ift . . ." repeated

GL (as in "<u>gl</u>ad")

Preoccupied with glamour and glitz . . .

Example is from: A Tribe Called Quest on "Glamour and Glitz"
Stutter technique: "gluh-gluh-gluh-gluh . . ." repeated

GR (as in "<u>gr</u>ow")

Their green grass is green, our green grass is brown . . .

Example is from: Mos Def on "Life in Marvelous Times"
Stutter technique: "gruh-gruh-gruh-gruh . . ." repeated

LB (as in "bu<u>lb</u>")

Speed of a bulb flash . . .

Example is from: Canibus on "Psych Evaluation"
Stutter technique: "ulb-ulb-ulb-ulb . . ." repeated

LD (as in "bui<u>ld</u>")

A child running wild from mild pressure . . .

Example is from: De La Soul's "Pony Ride"
Stutter technique: "ild-ild-ild-ild . . ." repeated

LF (as in "she<u>lf</u>")

Knowledge of self from off the shelf . . .

Example is from: GZA on "Swordsman"
Stutter technique: "ilf-ilf-ilf-ilf . . ." repeated

LK/LC (as in "si<u>lk</u>" or "ta<u>lc</u>")

Cold milk, bold silk . . .

Example is from: RZA on Ghostface Killah's "The Grain"
Stutter technique: "ilk-ilk-ilk-ilk . . ." repeated

LM (as in "fi<u>lm</u>")

The realm, hip-hop is to the helm, it's divine to hit the mind like slippery elms . . .

Example is from: Q-Tip on "Hey"
Stutter technique: "ilm-ilm-ilm-ilm . . ." repeated

LP (as in "hel**p**")

In my scalp, I'm higher than the Alps . . .

Example is from: Saafir on "Real Circus"
Stutter technique: "elp-elp-elp-elp . . ." repeated

LT (as in "bel**t**")

The cult, head-on assault, the result, death by the bolt . . .

Example is from: GZA on "Beneath the Surface"
Stutter technique: "elt-elt-elt-elt . . ." repeated

LTH (as in "hea**lth**")

My health, great with wealth, undetected like the wings of a Stealth . . .

Example is from: Prodigal Sunn on RZA's "The Whistle"
Stutter technique: "elth-elth-elth-elth . . ." repeated

MP (as in "sta**mp**")

Stomp, romp, stamp, amp, floor keep stepping . . .

Example is from: Leaders of the New School on "Classic Material"
Stutter technique: "amp-amp-amp-amp . . ." repeated

ND (as in "ha**nd**")

My friend, but I lend a hand helping . . .

Example is from: Del the Funky Homosapien on "Undisputed Champs"
Stutter technique: "and-and-and-and . . ." repeated

NK (as in "bli<u>nk</u>")

The man to thank, sharper than a shank, so don't try to rank, you get spanked point-blank . . .

Example is from: Lord Finesse on Trends of Culture's "Off & On (Freestylin' Mix)"
Stutter technique: "ink-ink-ink-ink . . ." repeated

NT (as in "hu<u>nt</u>")

Rap, hunt, stunt, front . . .

Example is from: Lil Wayne on B.G.'s "Fuck Big Boy"
Stutter technique: "unt-unt-unt-unt . . ." repeated

PL (as in "<u>pl</u>ay")

Platinum, pluck platinum plaques . . .

Example is from: Apathy on "Every Emcee"
Stutter technique: "pluh-pluh-pluh-pluh . . ." repeated

PR (as in "<u>pr</u>oud")

Crushing your pride by surprise, I be Sean Price . . .

Example is from: Sean Price on Boot Camp Clik's "Trading Places"
Stutter technique: "pruh-pruh-pruh-pruh . . ." repeated

PT (as in "scri<u>pt</u>")

I'm kept suspicious, I might have crept till you slept with fishes . . .

Example is from: Elzhi on Caltroit's "Goatit"
Stutter technique: "apt-apt-apt-apt . . ." repeated

SC/SK (as in "<u>sc</u>ale" or "<u>sk</u>ate")

I tell 'em scat, skittle, skibobble . . .

Example is from: Skee-Lo on "I Wish"
Stutter technique: "scuh-scuh-scuh-scuh . . ." repeated

SCR (as in "<u>scr</u>ape")

'Bout that scrilla scratch . . .

Example is from: Suga-T on E-40's "Lace Me Up"
Stutter technique: "scruh-scruh-scruh-scruh . . ." repeated

SL (as in "<u>sl</u>ide")

Slick and I slip and slide like a Slinky, slip and slide . . .

Example is from: Insane Clown Posse on "Beverly Kills"
Stutter technique: "sluh-sluh-sluh-sluh . . ." repeated

SM (as in "<u>sm</u>ile")

Smack the smile off a doubter . . .

Example is from: 3rd Bass on "Wordz of Wizdom"
Stutter technique: "smuh-smuh-smuh-smuh . . ." repeated

SN (as in "<u>sn</u>eak")

A snap, a snare, and a clap . . .

Example is from: Cashis on Eminem's "Syllables"
Stutter technique: "snuh-snuh-snuh-snuh . . ." repeated

SP (as in "<u>sp</u>ort")

When I speak I spit, when I spit what I spat, it splits your clique, spit, spat, speak, spoke . . .

Example is from: KRS-One on "Alright with Me"
Stutter technique: "spuh-spuh-spuh-spuh . . ." repeated

SPH (as in "<u>sph</u>inx")

We robbed the Sphinx . . .

Example is from: Clipse on "Taiwan to Texas"
Stutter technique: "sphuh-sphuh-sphuh-sphuh . . ."
  repeated

SPL (as in "splash")

This split-second splash . . .

Example is from: U-God on Wu-Tang Clan's "Diesel"
Stutter technique: "spluh-spluh-spluh-spluh . . ." repeated

SPR (as in "spring")

Lay away and spray away and spree away . . .

Example is from: Snoop Dogg on "My Own Way"
Stutter technique: "spruh-spruh-spruh-spruh . . ." repeated

SQU (as in "squeeze")

Squeeze till they squirm . . .

Example is from: Sporty Thievz on "Hitmen"
Stutter technique: "squh-squh-squh-squh . . ." repeated

ST (as in "start")

Stutter, step, stop, then move . . .

Example is from: Twista on "Yellow Light"
Stutter technique: "stuh-stuh-stuh-stuh . . ." repeated

STR (as in "strong")

I struggle and strive 'cause I'm told only the strong survive . . .

Example is from: Cocoa Brovaz on "Myah Angelow"
Stutter technique: "struh-struh-struh-struh . . ." repeated

SW (as in "sweet")

I swore, I swear we will always . . .

Example is from: Obie Trice on "Hands on You"
Stutter technique: "swuh-swuh-swuh-swuh . . ." repeated

TR (as in "<u>tr</u>ack")

Certain tricks of the trade to try . . .

Example is from: The Coup on "Underdogs"
Stutter technique: "truh-truh-truh-truh . . ." repeated

TW (as in "<u>tw</u>ist")

Twenty-four twelve gauges, pointing at twelve faces . . .

Example is from: Camu Tao on Vakill's "Forbidden Scriptures"
Stutter technique: "twuh-twuh-twuh-twuh . . ." repeated

X/CKS (as in "fle<u>x</u>" or "ki<u>cks</u>")

The context and then next, then flex and throw a hex on your whole complex . . .

Example is from: EPMD on "Get the Bozack"
Stutter technique: "ex-ex-ex-ex . . ." repeated

Vowel Sounds

A (as in "<u>A</u>meric<u>a</u>")

My daughter want another sister or a brother and you looking like a mother. I took you from a clubber to a lover . . .

Example is from: Lil Wayne on "Receipt"
Stutter technique: "uh-uh-uh-uh . . ." repeated

A (as in "c<u>a</u>t")

I'ma attack smack and make 'em stand back, black, strong as cognac, I got the knack . . .

Example is from: LL Cool J, "Nitro"
Stutter technique: "at-at-at-at . . ." repeated

AR (as in "p<u>ar</u>t")

I'm heartless, when it comes to having the back of my part-ners, yeah, we artists, but testing us ain't the smartest . . .

Example is from: Queen Latifah, "Elements I'm Among"
Stutter technique: "ar-ar-ar-ar . . ." repeated

EA/EE (as in "r<u>ea</u>d")

I come to teach and preach and reach in each. With the speech every leech I'll impeach . . .

Example is from: Big Daddy Kane on "Wrath of Kane"
Stutter technique: "ee-ee-ee-ee . . ." repeated

E (as in "m<u>e</u>n")

The best, oh yes, I guess suggest the rest should fess don't mess or test your highness . . .

Example is from: Big Daddy Kane on "Ain't No Half Steppin'"
Stutter technique: "en-en-en-en . . ." repeated

I (as in "s<u>i</u>t")

Dead in the middle of Little Italy, little did we know that we riddled some middlemen who didn't do diddly . . .

Example is from: Big Pun on "Twinz (Deep Cover '98)"
Stutter technique: "id-id-id-id . . ." repeated

OO (as in "b<u>oo</u>k")

My book of rhymes got 'em cooking, boy. This crooked mind of mines got 'em all shook and scared to look in my eyes . . .

Example is from: Eminem on Lil Wayne's "Drop the World"
Stutter technique: "look-look-look-look . . ." repeated

OO (as in "t<u>oo</u>")

I ruin all those I'm doing, I pursue 'em, make 'em boo and come to, you and your crew . . .

Example is from: Run DMC, "Bounce"
Stutter technique: "you-you-you-you . . ." repeated

OR (as in "w<u>ord</u>")

Then swerve serve words with nerve embedded, I said it, word. Damn, you nerd, man, you heard . . .

Example is from: Naughty by Nature's "Feel Me Flow"
Stutter technique: "erd-erd-erd-erd . . ." repeated

OR (as in "s<u>ort</u>")

Step inside my fort and get caught, with the trey pound shorter left on the sidewalks of New York . . .

Example is from: Kool G Rap on Frankie Cutlass's "Know Da Game"
Stutter technique: "ort-ort-ort-ort . . ." repeated

O (as in "n<u>o</u>t")

The Glock cocker, the block locker, the rock chopper, the shot popper, the jock cock blocker . . .

Example is from: Smoothe Da Hustler on "Broken Language"
Stutter technique: "hot-hot-hot-hot . . ." repeated

U (as in "b<u>u</u>t")

Bum stiggedy, bum stiggedy, bum, hon, I got that old pa-rum pa-pum-pum . . .

Example is from: Das EFX on "They Want EFX"
Stutter technique: "um-um-um-um . . ." repeated

Vowel Combinations

Sometimes vowels are placed together to create a blend of two sounds (technically called "diphthongs"). For example, "ERE" as in "here" uses the "E" and "A" sounds together. Although these sounds have been covered individually in the previous list, it is good to practice the combinations, as many of them are used frequently.

AY (as in "d<u>ay</u>")

Remain sane, no dame games, came from bane, to a changed man . . .

Example is from: Tech N9ne, "This Ring"
Stutter technique: "ay-ay-ay-ay . . ." repeated

EAR (as in "w<u>ear</u>")

Debonaire with flair, I scare, wear, and tear, without a care, running shit as if I was a mayor . . .

Example is from: Dr. Dre on "Keep Their Heads Ringin'"
Stutter technique: "air-air-air-air . . ." repeated

ERE (as in "h<u>ere</u>")

With all sincereness, I spit lyrics with raw severeness, gladiator fearless, Tyson style, leave 'em earless . . .

Example is from: The Lady of Rage, "Unfucwitable"
Stutter technique: "here-here-here-here . . ." repeated

O (as in "g<u>o</u>")

Get blown at home or whatever zone you roam, get two

flown to your dome, blow chromosomes out your flesh and bones . . .

Example is from: Kool G Rap on Frankie Cutlass's "Know Da Game"

Stutter technique: "oh-oh-oh-oh . . ." repeated

OUR (as in "t<u>our</u>," "n<u>ewer</u>")

Clog up your sewer, peep the maneuver, drop the ill manure . . .

Example is from: Jeru the Damaja on "D. Original"

Stutter technique: "ewer-ewer-ewer-ewer . . ." repeated

OW (as in "h<u>ow</u>")

Moving cowardness out of this, never out powerless, devour this and now it is . . .

Example is from: Slick Rick, "Impress the Kid"

Stutter technique: "how-how-how-how . . ." repeated

OY (as in "b<u>oy</u>")

It's your boy Rapper Noyd, clapping toys, leave you famous. Kill the noise, Zoid, you will get destroyed . . .

Example is from: Big Noyd on "Heartless"

Stutter technique: "oy-oy-oy-oy . . ." repeated

Y (as in "m<u>y</u>")

Light bright white, Simple Life white, nice life, knife fight white, Great White Hype white, Uncle Ben's rice white . . .

Example is from: R.A. the Rugged Man, "Black and White"

Stutter technique: "eye-eye-eye-eye . . ." repeated

Final Words

*Real hip-hop is always gonna be there, people that are
here for the art are always gonna be there.*
◄ Planet Asia ►

RBX

I like to hear rap—when I hear a brother really getting up and
getting his rhyme on, that's what I'm about. I'm not so much
about the quick gimmicks and the catchy, trendy, hot shit.
I [like] to hear a brother honing his craft and put his time
and work in and you can hear it and that's what should be
respected.

Vast Aire, Cannibal Ox

You could be saying something degrading, but if the flow is
great, everyone is gonna listen to it. And you can be saying
something that's worthwhile and great and positive, but if
the flow was cheesy and wack, no one's gonna listen to it.

R.A. the Rugged Man

Stay in those ciphers, stay in the studio, stay in the studio
nonstop, like non-fucking-stop. Don't do this as a part-time
gig, where you're in the studio once every six months. You
gotta be there nonstop and stay writing and stay competi-
tive, because the whole entire fucking world wants to do

what you're doing, so if you're mediocre [then] there's no room for you, you don't deserve to be here. So just stay doing what you're doing, nonstop, it's like anything, you know.

Termanology

My advice would be to go back in history and listen. Go listen. Don't be dumb, don't be dumb to your culture, go back and listen. Any basketball player coming up right now definitely knows who Michael Jordan is, so if you're starting to rap right now and you don't know who Rakim is, c'mon, man, you gotta go back, you gotta buy that album, go find out who Rakim is. Go listen to that *Illmatic* CD, that first Nas and *Reasonable Doubt*, that first Jay-Z. Go listen to all that shit, man, that's what real hip-hop is. If you ain't doing it like that, whatever, man, you're just another cat, that's it, you ain't never gonna be nobody special.

Myka 9, Freestyle Fellowship

Some things change, some things stay the same. I don't think that any real tenet of MCs or hip-hop has died out yet, because people love it so much they make sure that most of it's pure. But there was a more mythological sort of stance and more of a sensei sort of vibration that earlier MCs that came to fame and came to knowledge had. It's almost like a path to enlightenment in the sense of being exposed to so many ideas through lyrics that you start to do your own research and I guess expose yourself to new and different things. So in a way rap is an educational tool, I was able to get to college just by the same thought patterns I used in hip-hop.

Akir

The most important thing that helped me get to where I am now is knowing the opportunity that I have to test-market music, and knowing how valuable that is. Don't be scared to go and do shows, don't be scared to stand out on the corner and sell your music, don't be scared to let people, especially strangers, hear your music. Your friends—hopefully you have friends that will tell you the truth, but no matter what, they have a biased opinion, because they're talking to their friend. There's nothing like talking to a stranger, talking or playing your stuff to a stranger, because they're gonna give you a raw aspect on it, because they have no emotional tie to you.

Masta Ace

I think it's just like back in the days—you got guys that do it at a high level, and you got guys that are terrible, it's no different today. And for whatever it's worth, the skill level does not dictate at all the record sales. Record sales have nothing to do with having talent, having ability. It's a whole different ballgame when you start talking about selling records.

Bobby Creekwater

Today's MCs—this is my only gripe—I just wish a lot more MCs would come into it with their own identity. I think MCs of the past, everybody had their own niche and their own thing and nowadays you get some MCs going for the same approach or doing the same type of music. Even if it's subconscious, they end up doing the same type of music. Back when everybody was on their own thing, it was exciting because of it, so that's my only gripe, but other than that, man, everybody's good with me.

Planet Asia

As far as MCing goes, you have to obtain knowledge in order to rhyme, you have to have knowledge. That's why I stress reading [and] being a good observer . . . being a good fan, a listener first, know what you're getting into. This is hip-hop—know it, get acquainted with it.

Interviewed Artists

The following is a list of all the artists who have been quoted in *How to Rap 2* (from the exclusive *How to Rap* interviews conducted for the first book) with brief descriptions of each, in alphabetical order.

Aesop Rock

A critically acclaimed MC who has released albums on the esteemed Definitive Jux record label, Aesop Rock is one of the most notable figures in hip-hop's underground. He has collaborated with many other underground artists and groups, including MF Doom, Vast Aire, Mr. Lif, MURS, Rjd2, Blockhead, Zion I, Cage, El-P, and Percee P.

Akil the MC, Jurassic 5

The alternative hip-hop group Jurassic 5 is one of the most popular acts to emerge from the independent scene. They have several critically acclaimed albums and have collaborated with Linkin Park, Nelly Furtado, Dave Matthews Band, Dilated Peoples, and Blackalicious, among others. They formally disbanded in 2007, but their members still tour and have released solo material.

Akir

Akir is a well-respected underground rapper known for his intricate lyrics and politically aware content, as well as his close association with acclaimed rapper Immortal Technique.

Andy Cat, Ugly Duckling

The members of Californian independent hip-hip group Ugly Duckling are known for their humorous and intelligent lyrics, as well as the old-school influences that inform their sound. They have released several acclaimed albums and EPs and are one of the most prominent underground hip-hop groups.

B-Real, Cypress Hill

Cypress Hill is one of the most well-known and acclaimed West Coast groups in hip-hop. They have sold over 9 million records and are known for their first three classic albums and signature songs, such as "Insane in the Brain," "Dr. Greenthumb," and "Rap Superstar." They have worked with Eminem, Wu-Tang Clan, OutKast, Dr. Dre, and N.O.R.E., among many others.

Big Daddy Kane

One of the most influential and well-respected MCs ever, Big Daddy Kane is often featured in the top 10 of many "greatest MCs of all time" lists, including lists by MTV and Kool Moe Dee. He has collaborated with Jay-Z (who was Big Daddy Kane's hype man), Busta Rhymes, Public Enemy, 2Pac, Big L, UGK, Q-Tip, Jurassic 5, and others.

Big Noyd

A close affiliate of Mobb Deep who is featured on many of the group's albums, including the classics *The Infamous* and *Juvenile Hell*, Big Noyd is known for his agile flow and hard-core lyricism. He has also featured on tracks alongside Nas and Rakim.

Big Pooh, Little Brother

Josh Dehonney

Little Brother is one of the most critically acclaimed underground hip-hop groups, known for conscious lyrics and concept albums. Their first two albums were produced by Grammy Award–winning producer 9th Wonder, who was previously part of the group and has also produced for such artists as Mary J. Blige, Jay-Z, and Destiny's Child. They have also collaborated with such artists as Lil Wayne and MURS. They formally disbanded in 2010 to pursue solo projects.

Bishop Lamont

A protégé of Dr. Dre (whose previous protégés include Eminem, 50 Cent, and Snoop Dogg), he has collaborated with many of the biggest names in hip-hop, such as Busta Rhymes, Dr. Dre, and Warren G, among others. He is known for his often humorous and confrontational lyrics.

Bobby Creekwater

One of a select number of rappers to have been signed to Eminem's Shady Records label, Bobby Creekwater is a popular southern MC who has released several acclaimed mixtapes, and who was featured on Eminem's 2006 Shady Records mixtape LP *The Re-Up*, which has sold over 1 million copies.

Boot Camp Clik (Sean Price, Heltah Skeltah; Buckshot, Black Moon)

Legendary Boot Camp Clik groups Black Moon, Heltah Skeltah, and Smif N Wessun have all released classic hip-hop albums, have sold over 3 million records together, and continue to release highly respected records. They are known for their intricate yet rugged flows and have worked with numerous renowned artists such as 2Pac, Busta Rhymes, and M.O.P.

Bootie Brown, The Pharcyde

See "The Pharcyde."

Brother Ali

Signed to the acclaimed label Rhymesayers, Brother Ali is known for his intelligent lyrics, agile flow, and expressive voice, and he has released several critically revered underground albums, often featuring production from Atmosphere producer Ant. His lyrics regularly include political themes and socially conscious subjects.

Brother J, X Clan

Devin DeHaven, courtesy
Suburban Noize Records

X Clan is a conscious hip-hop group whose debut album, *To the East, Blackwards*, is considered a classic and was included in *The Source* magazine's 100 Best Rap Albums. They have collaborated with Jurassic 5, KRS-One, and Jacoby Shaddix of the rock band Papa Roach.

Buckshot, Black Moon

Robert Adam Mayer

See "Boot Camp Clik."

Cage

Cage has released albums on the respected Definitive Jux label and is known for his poetic and intelligent lyrics, as well as his earlier horror-core albums. He has also collaborated with many esteemed underground artists, including Aesop Rock, El-P, and Necro.

Cappadonna, Wu-Tang Clan affiliate

Very closely aligned with Wu-Tang Clan, one of the most successful and widely recognized groups in hip-hop, Cappadonna has appeared on several classic Wu-Tang albums—being especially heavily featured on *Wu-Tang Forever*, which sold over 8 million copies—as well as on two of Wu-Tang's most praised LPs—Raekwon's *Only Built 4 Cuban Linx* (over 1 million sold) and Ghostface Killah's *Ironman* (over 1 million sold)—and many other Wu-Tang releases. His classic debut LP, *The Pillage*, sold over half a million copies.

Chuck D, Public Enemy

Sarah Edwards

Public Enemy is one of the most influential groups, in hip-hop and outside of it, of all time, often included in "best" and "greatest" lists by *Rolling Stone*, *The Source*, *XXL*, MTV, VH1, and others. Chuck D is known for his insightful, confrontational, and often politically oriented lyrics, as well as for having one of the most recognizable voices in music. They have sold around 5 million records, and their album *It Takes a Nation of Millions to Hold Us Back* is often referred to in publications such as *NME*, *Vibe*, and *Q* as the greatest hip-hop album ever.

Crooked I

Crooked I is a West Coast artist known for his exceptional MCing skills and lyrical dexterity. He is a member of the hip-hop supergroup Slaughterhouse, alongside Royce Da 5'9", Joell Ortiz, and Joe Budden, and has collaborated with, among others, Luniz and Akon. He has released numerous acclaimed mixtapes and freestyles.

David Banner

David Banner is a southern MC who has sold over 1 million records and has had several hit singles, including "Play," which reached #7 on the Billboard Hot 100 singles chart in 2005. He has worked with many of the biggest names in hip-hop, including Snoop Dogg, Akon, and Lil Wayne, all of whom were featured on his 2007 song "9mm." He is also known as a philanthropist and actor, having starred alongside Samuel L. Jackson and Christina Ricci in the film *Black Snake Moan*.

Del the Funky Homosapien

Scott Stewart

Del is an esteemed West Coast rapper, is a member of the Hieroglyphics crew, is Ice Cube's cousin, and is known for his distinct style, intelligent lyrics, and classic catalog. He was also featured on the self-titled debut album of Gorillaz, with Damon Albarn of Blur, and rapped on the group's hit single "Clint Eastwood."

Devin the Dude

Devin the Dude is a cult favorite who regularly collaborates with the biggest names in hip-hop, such as Snoop Dogg, Jay-Z, Dr. Dre, Lil Wayne, Ice Cube, André 3000 of OutKast, Scarface, Xzibit, the Roots, Lil Jon, De La Soul, Chamillionaire, and Nas. He is also famous for his guest appearance on Dr. Dre's classic *2001* album (10 million copies sold), which led to him being part of the Up in Smoke Tour with Eminem, Dr. Dre, Snoop Dogg, Xzibit, and Ice Cube.

Dray, Das EFX

Dray is one-half of Das EFX, known for their lyrical creativity and the influential vocal style they pioneered in the early 1990s. Their debut album, *Dead Serious*, is a hip-hop classic, included in *The Source* magazine's 100 Best Rap Albums, and their first three albums reached #16, #20, and #22 on the Billboard Top 200 albums chart—they have sold over 1.5 million records.

E-40

E-40 has sold well over 3 million records; has had six albums in the Top 20 of Billboard Top 200 albums chart, including a #3 in 2006; and has had several hit singles, such as "Tell Me When to Go" and "U and Dat." E-40 is known for his agile flow and expressive delivery. He appeared on 2Pac's *All Eyez on Me* LP, which sold 9 million copies, and has worked with Ice Cube, Bone Thugs-N-Harmony, and Too $hort.

El Da Sensei

Underground MC and part of New Jersey–based Artifacts—whose debut album, *Between a Rock and a Hard Place*, was an underground favorite—El Da Sensei is also known for his intelligent lyrics and raw, uncompromising approach. He has worked with Brand Nubian, Pharoahe Monch, J-Live, O.C. of Diggin' in the Crates, and Sean Price, among others.

Josh Dehonney

Esoteric

Esoteric is one-half of the well-respected underground duo 7L & Esoteric. They have worked with many other hip-hop artists, such as Inspectah Deck of Wu-Tang Clan, Jedi Mind Tricks, Apathy, Celph Titled, and Outerspace, and are also members of the underground hip-hop supergroups the Demigodz and Army of the Pharaohs.

Diana Levine

Evidence, Dilated Peoples

One of the most notable groups to come out of hip-hop's independent scene, Dilated Peoples have released several acclaimed albums and have collaborated with Cypress Hill, Kanye West, Devin the Dude, Aceyalone, Planet Asia, the Alchemist, DJ Premier, the Roots, Gang Starr, the Beatnuts, Tha Alkaholiks, and others.

Fredro Starr, Onyx

Fredro Starr is a rapper in the group Onyx, who have released several classic albums and sold over 2 million records—they are best known for their hit single "Slam." They have had three albums in the Top 25 of the Billboard Top 200 albums chart, and their debut album, *Bacdafucup*, was selected as one of *The Source* magazine's 100 Best Rap Albums. Fredro has also had two acclaimed solo albums and is an actor who has starred in major films such as *Clockers, Sunset Park, Ride, Light It Up*, and *Save the Last Dance* and appeared in TV roles on such shows as *Moesha, The Wire, NYPD Blue, Law & Order, Blade: The Series*, and *Promised Land*.

Gift of Gab, Blackalicious

Gift of Gab is the MC in the group Blackalicious, on Quannum Records. They are noted for their intelligent and intricate lyrics and music, have worked with revered producer DJ Shadow, and are one of the most popular groups in the independent hip-hop scene. Gift of Gab is also known for his tongue-twisting flow.

Guerilla Black

Guerilla Black is a West Coast rapper from Compton, California, who is often noted for his similarity in style and appearance to deceased hip-hop legend the Notorious B.I.G. His acclaimed debut album, *Guerilla City*, reached #20 on the Billboard Top 200 albums chart, and he has also released several well-received mixtapes.

Hell Rell, Dipset

Hell Rell is a member of the Diplomats (Dipset) crew and has appeared on numerous popular Diplomats records that have collectively sold in the millions. He has also released several successful solo albums that have appeared on the Billboard charts.

Ill Bill

Ill Bill is a hard-core MC who is part of underground favorites Non Phixion. He is known for the political nature of his lyrics, has released acclaimed albums, and is part of the group La Coka Nostra, along with Everlast, Danny Boy, and DJ Lethal, all of House of Pain. He has also worked with Vinnie Paz, B-Real, Immortal Technique, Tech N9ne, and Raekwon, among others.

Mike McRath

Imani, The Pharcyde

See "The Pharcyde."

Immortal Technique

Carey Stuart

Immortal Technique is an acclaimed MC and political activist with confrontational lyrics often dealing with political themes. He has collaborated with a number of other MCs, including Crooked I, Pharoahe Monch, Akir, Chino XL, Ras Kass, and Jean Grae.

Killah Priest, Wu-Tang Clan affiliate

Killah Priest is one of the most respected rappers associated with the Wu-Tang Clan since his appearance on GZA's album *Liquid Swords* (over 500,000 copies sold), which included Killah Priest's classic solo track "B.I.B.L.E." He is also featured on GZA's *Beneath the Surface* (over 500,000 sold), and on Ol' Dirty Bastard's *Return to the 36 Chambers* (over 500,000 sold). His debut album, *Heavy Mental*, is considered a hip-hop classic and reached #24 on the Billboard Top 200 albums chart.

Kool G Rap

Kool G Rap is one of the most influential MCs of all time, with Eminem, Jay-Z, Big Pun, R.A. the Rugged Man, and many others citing him among their influences. He is frequently on "greatest MCs of all time" lists, and is featured in the Top 15 of Kool Moe Dee's book *There's a God on the Mic: The True 50 Greatest MCs*. His techniques are evident in many of the most acclaimed MCs' lyrics, and he has appeared on tracks with numerous artists, including Eminem, Nas, AZ, Mobb Deep, Busta Rhymes, Big L, Ghostface Killah, and Canibus.

K-Os

K-Os is a Canadian rapper known for his conscious lyrics and for incorporating various styles of music such as funk, rock, and reggae. All his albums have been well received, and *Atlantis: Hymns for Disco* debuted at #1 on the Canadian charts. He has also collaborated with the Chemical Brothers (on the track "Get Yourself High") and others.

The Lady of Rage

Considered one of the most skillful female MCs, the Lady of Rage has appeared on some of the most highly rated West Coast albums, such as Dr. Dre's *The Chronic* (3 million sold), Snoop Dogg's *Doggystyle* (4 million), Tha Dogg Pound's *Dogg Food* (2 million), and the soundtrack album for the film *Above the Rim* (2 million). She is known for her mastery of flow and her hard-core lyrics.

Lateef, Latyrx

Lateef is half of the acclaimed duo Latyrx (along with Lyrics Born) as well as a member of the Quannum collective along with Blackalicious, DJ Shadow, and others. Lateef featured on Fatboy Slim's hit singles "That Old Pair of Jeans" and "Wonderful Night," and he has also appeared on two of DJ Shadow's singles.

Lord Jamar, Brand Nubian

Alternative hip-hop group Brand Nubian are known for their socially conscious lyrics and classic albums. Their debut album, *One for All*, received the highest rating possible in *The Source* magazine and was included in the magazine's 100 Best Rap Albums. Group member Lord Jamar is also an actor, best known for his role of Supreme Allah on the TV series *Oz*. He has also appeared on *The Sopranos*, *Law & Order: Special Victims Unit*, and *Third Watch*.

Masta Ace

A highly respected MC with a long career, Masta Ace has consistently put out acclaimed releases from the 1980s to the present day. He is frequently on "greatest MCs of all time" lists, and is featured in Kool Moe Dee's book *There's a God on the Mic: The True 50 Greatest MCs*. He is part of the Juice Crew, the famous late-1980s hip-hop collective, along with several other of the most highly rated MCs in hip-hop history.

MC Shan

MC Shan is part of the legendary late-1980s hip-hop collective the Juice Crew. *The Source* magazine ranked his 1988 debut, *Down by Law*, as one of the 100 Best Rap Albums of all time, and he is featured in Kool Moe Dee's book *There's a God on the Mic: The True 50 Greatest MCs*.

Mighty Casey

Mighty Casey is an underground artist from Boston, best known for his humorous lyrics and his song "White Girls," which was in rotation on cable network BET and was also used in the film *White Chicks*, a popular comedy by the Wayans brothers.

Mr. Lif

Mr. Lif is an MC who has released records on renowned record label Definitive Jux and is known for the political content and intelligence in his lyrics. He is also a member of the hip-hop group the Perceptionists (with Akrobatik) and has released several acclaimed albums and EPs.

MURS

Releasing albums through Warner Bros. Records and the Definitive Jux record label, MURS is known for his insightful and intelligent lyrics. He is a member of several hip-hop collectives, such as Living Legends, Felt, and 3 Melancholy Gypsys, and has worked with Snoop Dogg, DJ Quik, and will.i.am of Black Eyed Peas.

Myka 9, Freestyle Fellowship

Daniel Solomon

Myka 9 is part of the influential underground Californian group Freestyle Fellowship, known for their expert freestyling techniques and for incorporating elements of jazz into their music. Their early albums are considered hip-hop classics, and they continue to put out highly acclaimed and boundary-pushing material.

Nelly

Grammy Award–winner Nelly has sold over 20 million records, as well as numerous Top 10 hits, including four that reached #1 on the Billboard Hot 100 chart and three #1 albums on the Billboard Top 200 albums chart. He has worked with T.I., Lil Wayne, Snoop Dogg, LL Cool J, Akon, Chuck D, the Neptunes, Fat Joe, Remy Ma, Mobb Deep, and Missy Elliot, among others.

O.C., Diggin' in the Crates

O.C. is part of the Diggin' in the Crates (DITC) crew and is known for his widely acclaimed debut album, *Word . . . Life*, and for commanding great respect as an MC, especially from fellow rappers and long-time hip-hop fans. He has worked with Pharoahe Monch, Lord Finesse, Fat Joe, Big L, Buckwild, Sadat X, Chubb Rock, Jeru the Damaja, and others.

Omar Cruz

Omar Cruz is a West Coast MC who was signed jointly to major labels Interscope and Geffen Records. His street album, *The Cruzifixion*, received the highest possible rating from *Scratch* magazine. He has worked with some of the most esteemed hip-hop producers, such as Cool & Dre, Hi-Tek, Nottz, and DJ Khalil, and collaborated with West Coast favorites the Game and WC.

One Be Lo, Binary Star

Part of the group Binary Star, One Be Lo is known for his conscious and intelligent lyrics and for Binary Star's debut album, *Water World*, which is highly regarded among fans of underground hip-hop. One Be Lo has also released a number of acclaimed solo albums.

The Pharcyde (Bootie Brown and Imani)

The Pharcyde is a West Coast group known for their canonical debut album, *Bizarre Ride II the Pharcyde*, which sold over 500,000 copies, as well as their conscious and often humorous content. Bootie Brown also rapped on a single from the album *Demon Days* by Gorillaz, an album that sold over 2 million copies.

Pharoahe Monch

One of hip-hop's most well-respected MCs, Pharoahe Monch is known for his complex lyricism and mastery of flow. He has released acclaimed solo albums, as well as classic LPs as part of the group Organized Konfusion, and has worked with Q-Tip, Mos Def, Nate Dogg, De La Soul, Kool G Rap, O.C. of DITC, Talib Kweli, DJ Quik, Ras Kass, Canibus, Macy Gray, and many others.

Pigeon John

Pigeon John is an L.A. rapper who is also part of the group L.A. Symphony. He is signed to the Quannum label along with Blackalicious, Lyrics Born, Lateef, and Lifesavas. Known for his often humorous and positive lyrics, he has released numerous well-respected albums.

Planet Asia

Shemp "The Photo Doctor"

Planet Asia is a Grammy-nominated underground rapper who has been awarded the Independent Album of the Year award twice by *The Source* magazine. He has collaborated with artists such as Linkin Park, Talib Kweli, Bun B, and Ghostface Killah, among others, and is known for his versatility and intelligent lyrics.

Pusha-T, Clipse

Clipse have several widely acclaimed albums, two of which were entirely produced by the Neptunes, including their hit single "Grindin." They have sold over 750,000 records, with two of their albums reaching #4 and #14 on the Billboard Top 200 albums chart. *XXL* gave their 2006 album *Hell Hath No Fury* its highest review rating, only the sixth album to receive the rating in the magazine's history. They have collaborated with Justin Timberlake (on his hit single "Like I Love You"), Kelis, Nelly, the Game, Fabolous, and Faith Evans, among others.

Q-Tip, A Tribe Called Quest

One of the most influential groups in hip-hop, A Tribe Called Quest have sold over 4 million records as a group, and their members have also released successful solo albums. They have had three albums in the Top 10 of the Billboard Top 200 albums chart and are respected critically for their first three classic albums. They have collaborated with, and produced for, artists such as Mobb Deep, Jay-Z, Kanye West, Pharrell Williams, Nas, Busta Rhymes, the Beastie Boys, Black Eyed Peas, DJ Shadow, De La Soul, the Roots, Common, Mos Def, Janet Jackson, Mariah Carey, R.E.M., the Chemical Brothers, and Whitney Houston.

R.A. the Rugged Man

One of the most skillful lyricists in hip-hop, R.A. the Rugged Man has worked with legends such as the Notorious B.I.G., Mobb Deep, Tragedy Khadafi, and Wu-Tang Clan. He was also a contributor to *Ego Trip's Book of Rap Lists* and *Ego Trip's Big Book of Racism*, and has written articles for popular magazines such as *Vibe*, *King*, and *The Source*.

Rah Digga

Formerly part of Busta Rhymes's Flipmode Squad, Rah Digga is one of hip-hop's most skilled female MCs, appearing on the Fugees' *The Score* (6 million sold) and numerous Busta Rhymes albums. She also released an acclaimed solo album, *Dirty Harriet*, which went to #18 on the Billboard Top 200 albums chart.

Rampage, Flipmode Squad

Part of Busta Rhymes's Flipmode Squad, Rampage has appeared on six Busta Rhymes albums (combined sales of over 5 million). He was featured on Craig Mack's "Flava in Ya Ear Remix," widely regarded as one of the greatest posse cuts in hip-hop history, as well as on Busta Rhymes's classic single "Woo Hah!! Got You All in Check." He has also released several successful solo albums.

RBX

RBX has had memorable guest appearances on some of hip-hop's most influential and lauded albums, such as Eminem's *The Marshall Mathers LP* (9 million sold), Snoop Dogg's *Doggystyle* (4 million), and Dr. Dre's *The Chronic* (3 million). He also ghostwrote Dre's Grammy-winning hit single "Let Me Ride" and has released several well-respected solo LPs.

Royce Da 5'9"

Well-respected lyricist Royce Da 5'9" is part of the duo Bad Meets Evil with long-time friend Eminem—their 2011 album *Hell: The Sequel* reached #1 on the Billboard Top 200 albums chart. He has ghostwritten for Dr. Dre and P. Diddy and is part of the hip-hop supergroup Slaughterhouse. He is known for his intricate flow and wordplay, has released several well-received albums and mixtapes, and has also collaborated with DJ Premier, the Neptunes, Clipse, and Twista, among others.

Schoolly D

Otto van den Toorn

Schoolly D is an influential MC who debuted in the mid-1980s and is often credited with inventing gangsta rap. He has a number of classic tracks that have been sampled and referenced by countless other hip-hop artists, such as "P.S.K. What Does It Mean?" "Gucci Time," and "Saturday Night," and his album *Saturday Night—The Album* was included in *The Source* magazine's 100 Best Rap Albums. He also wrote the theme music for the popular TV show *Aqua Teen Hunger Force*.

Sean Price, Heltah Skeltah

See "Boot Camp Clik."

Alexander Richter

Shock G, Digital Underground

Shock G is the lead rapper of Digital Underground, who have sold over 3.5 million records and released several classic albums, with their debut album, *Sex Packets*, being included in *The Source* magazine's 100 Best Rap Albums list. They are also noted for launching the career of 2Pac—Shock G produced numerous tracks for 2Pac during his career.

Heather Christianson

Speech, Arrested Development

Speech is the lead rapper of Arrested Development, a progressive hip-hop group whose classic debut, *3 Years, 5 Months & 2 Days in the Life of . . .*, won them two Grammys, and who have sold over 5 million records. Their song "Tennessee" is part of the Rock and Roll Hall of Fame's 500 Songs That Shaped Rock and Roll list.

Stat Quo

Stat Quo is a southern MC who was signed jointly to Eminem and Dr. Dre's record labels—Shady and Aftermath, respectively. He has appeared on various Eminem projects, such as the *Encore* album and *The Re-Up*, and has worked extensively with Dr. Dre, as well as collaborating with Young Buck, 50 Cent, Obie Trice, Cashis, Bobby Creekwater, Rah Digga, and others.

Stressmatic, The Federation

The Federation is a popular Bay Area hip-hop group on Warner Bros. Records produced exclusively by Rick Rock, who has produced for other artists such as 2Pac, Jay-Z, Busta Rhymes, Method Man, and Will Smith. As a group they have collaborated with Snoop Dogg, Travis Barker of rock band blink-182, E-40, and others.

T3, Slum Village

Slum Village is an acclaimed Detroit hip-hop group who had a hit single with "Selfish," produced by Kanye West and featuring John Legend. They are also known for working extensively with the late J Dilla, who was originally part of the group and is regarded as one of the best hip-hop producers of all time.

Tajai, Souls of Mischief

Souls of Mischief is part of the Hieroglyphics crew, along with Del the Funky Homosapien and others. They are noted for their classic debut album, *93 'Til Infinity*, which was included in *The Source* magazine's 100 Best Rap Albums, as well as for consistently releasing quality material as individual solo artists and as a group.

Tash, Tha Alkaholiks

Tha Alkaholiks, one of the most notable groups on the West Coast, have had a series of respected albums as a group and as solo artists and are known for their humorous and skilled hard-core rhymes. They are also part of the Likwit Crew—with King Tee, Xzibit, Lootpack, and others—and have worked with Bishop Lamont, Busta Rhymes, Kurupt, Raekwon, B-Real, OutKast, and Q-Tip, among others.

Tech N9ne

Tech N9ne is known for his mastery of flow and intricate lyricism, and for being able to rap incredibly fast in a variety of complex rhythms. He has released numerous acclaimed albums and has appeared on tracks alongside Eminem, Kool G Rap, Pharoahe Monch, the RZA, KRS-One, Yukmouth, Brotha Lynch Hung, Ill Bill, Twista, Ice Cube, Scarface, X Clan, and many others.

Joshua Hoffine

Termanology

Known for his complex lyricism, Termanology has collaborated with many of the biggest names in hip-hop, including Nas, Royce Da 5'9", Papoose, M.O.P., Bun B, and Terror Squad. He also has the backing and production of legendary hip-hop producer DJ Premier, who has produced for Jay-Z, Snoop Dogg, Nas, the Notorious B.I.G., AZ, and Christina Aguilera.

Thes One, People Under the Stairs

West Coast group People Under the Stairs is one of the most prominent underground hip-hop groups. They have put out a number of acclaimed albums and EPs and are known for their conscious, positive content and dense, intricate production, which recalls hip-hop's golden age.

Twista

Twista, known as one of the fastest rappers ever, has sold over 3 million records. He had a #1 single on the Billboard Hot 100 chart with "Slow Jamz," as well as the hits "Girl Tonite" and "Overnight Celebrity." He has worked with Kanye West, the Neptunes, Jamie Foxx, T-Pain, R. Kelly, Mariah Carey, Trick Daddy, Cam'ron, and many others.

2Mex, The Visionaries

2Mex is part of the group the Visionaries, known for their positive lyrics and intricate rhymes. Their music has been featured in Warner Bros.' box-office hit *Oceans Twelve* and the MTV feature film *Volcano High*, and they have collaborated with numerous distinguished hip-hop artists and groups, including Brand Nubian, RBX, Dilated Peoples, and Brother J of X Clan.

Vast Aire, Cannibal Ox

Cannibal Ox is an underground hip-hop group whose debut album, *The Cold Vein*, produced by El-P, is one of the most acclaimed releases in independent rap. Vast Aire has worked with numerous other underground favorites, including Aesop Rock, C-Rayz Walz, and Cage.

Vinnie Paz, Jedi Mind Tricks

Mike McRath

Philadelphia hip-hop group Jedi Mind Tricks are known for their hard-core and intelligent approach and have collaborated with many of the most respected MCs in the genre, including Kool G Rap, Sean Price, Killah Priest, GZA, R.A. the Rugged Man, Tragedy Khadafi, Ras Kass, Canibus, Percee P, and Ill Bill.

Vursatyl, Lifesavas

Vursatyl is one-third of the group Lifesavas—known for their positive and introspective lyrics and intricate flows. They are signed to popular independent label Quannum, and they have collaborated with several notable artists such as DJ Shadow, Dead Prez, and Blackalicious.

Wise Intelligent, Poor Righteous Teachers

Known for its conscious lyrics, the debut album of Poor Righteous Teachers, *Holy Intellect*, was included in *The Source* magazine's 100 Best Rap Albums and is considered a hip-hop classic. They continually release acclaimed albums and have collaborated with the Fugees and KRS-One, among others.

Wordsworth

A well-respected underground rapper from Brooklyn, Wordsworth appeared on A Tribe Called Quest's *The Love Movement* and on Mos Def and Talib Kweli's album *Black Star*. He was also involved in MTV's comedy sketch series *Lyricist Lounge* and is part of supergroup eMC, with Masta Ace, Punchline, and Strick.

Pawel Fabjanski

Yukmouth

Yukmouth is a member of the group Luniz, whose debut album, *Operation Stackola*, sold over a million copies, and is known for the smash hit "I Got 5 on It." He has also sold over a million records as a solo artist, with his solo debut, *Thugged Out: The Albulation*, selling over 500,000 records, and he is known for his extensive list of collaborations with such fellow West Coast artists as the Game, E-40, and Shock G.

Zumbi, Zion I

Zion I is a renowned underground group, known for their intelligent, positive, and socially conscious lyrics. They have collaborated with other notable artists such as Talib Kweli, Aesop Rock, Del the Funky Homosapien, Gift of Gab, and others, and they have released a number of acclaimed albums.

Index